"If you've ever had the privilege o
son as I have, you'll find he is a man who knows how to pray.
In his new book, Charles teaches us practical ways to deepen
our prayer life, giving us a closer relationship with the Lord
Jesus."

Ricky Skaggs,
country/bluegrass artist

"This is some of the finest teaching on prayer I have ever read.
What makes it doubly good is having Charles share from his
personal story along the way—scriptural insights, experiencing
God's presence, lessons from everyday life—in which the ways
of prayer become a way of life."

Larry Christenson,
former director,
International Lutheran Renewal Center; author,
The Christian Family, The Mantle of Esther

"This book takes a unique approach to prayer. Through practical Biblical teaching and candid personal stories, Charles takes
you on a journey into knowing God through prayer. His honest
approach to prayer will refresh and renew you. If you are thirsty
for God's presence, this is a must-read."

Michael Coleman,
co-founder and former president, Integrity Media

"I have known Charles Simpson for over forty years. His godly
leadership in the Kingdom of God is without question. He skill-
fully weaves personal and practical experience with biblical
truth that sets this book apart from others on the great subject
of prayer and will challenge the reader."

Dick Iverson,
founder, Ministers Fellowship International

"What an excellent and godly book! Some writers have produced a volume of books on prayer. I believe this outstanding book by Charles Simpson will be the defining single book on the subject for the 21st century."

Charles Green,
president, Harvest Ministries to the World

"After fifteen-plus years in Christian music ministry, prayer for me is indispensable. Brother Charles' book on prayer has taken me to the next level in live connection with God. I highly recommend that any who are serious about their relationship with God avail themselves to the wisdom in this book."

Joseph Rojas, founder, Seventh Day Slumber

Straight Answers to 21 Honest Questions About PRAYER

© 2013 by Charles V. Simpson

Published by Chosen Books
11400 Hampshire Avenue South
Bloomington, Minnesota 55438
www.chosenbooks.com

Chosen Books is a division of
Baker Publishing Group, Grand Rapids, Michigan

Printed in the United States of America

Library of Congress Cataloging-in-Publication Data
Simpson, Charles, 1937–
    Straight answers to 21 honest questions about prayer / Charles Simpson.
        pages cm
    Includes bibliographical references.
    Summary: "This no-guilt approach answers 21 of the most common questions about prayer, including Does a prayer always work, How do you pray without ceasing? and more"—Provided by publisher.
    ISBN 978-0-8007-9566-5 (pbk. : alk. paper)
    1. Prayer—Christianity—Miscellanea. I. Title. II. Title: Straight answers to twenty-one honest questions about prayer.
BV210.3.S563 2013
248.3′2—dc23   2013017683

Cover design by Gearbox

13 14 15 16 17 18 19   7 6 5 4 3 2 1

Straight Answers to 21 Honest Questions About
PRAYER

CHARLES SIMPSON

Chosen
a division of Baker Publishing Group
www.ChosenBooks.com

This book is dedicated to John and Wendy Beckett. John is chairman of the Beckett Corporation and serves on the boards of a number of Christian ministries, such as Cru (Campus Crusade for Christ) and The King's College in New York City. He and Wendy are both authors.

John helped establish Intercessors for America in 1973, which has encouraged hundreds of thousands of people in their prayer lives. John also established an evangelistic website (lifesgreatestquestion.com), through which over two million have indicated decisions for Christ.

I have known John and Wendy since 1969. They have inspired me in my prayer life and walk with the Lord, as they have literally millions of others.

The world is in its condition not so much for a lack of prayer, but for a lack of effective prayer. It is not enough for us to say, "Pray more," without teaching how to pray as Jesus taught His disciples. But He did much more than teach them the words to pray: He taught them how to pray effectively—and that will be our quest.

Contents

Acknowledgments 11

1. What Is Prayer? 13

2. Who Am I Talking to Here? 22

3. Why Pray? 30

4. What Can I Learn from Jesus' Prayers? 40

5. Why Is Forgiveness So Important? 51

6. How Does God Want Me to Pray? 60

7. How Important Is Faith When I Pray? 68

8. What Does It Mean to Pray in the Holy Spirit? 77

9. What Does It Mean to Pray Fervently? 88

10. Is Prayer Worth the Labor? 99

11. How Does Righteousness Affect Our Prayers? 108

12. Should I Quote Scripture When I Pray? 114

13. Should I Expect to Hear from God? 121

14. Do I Have to Wait? 132

15. Is He Always on My Mind? 141

Contents

16. Do I Give Him a Blank Check?   147

17. What Do I Do When It Does Not Seem to Be
    Working?   153

18. I Believe I Have Heard the Lord—What Should I
    Do Now?   163

19. Should I Fast?   169

20. What Do You Mean by "the Manifest Presence
    of God"?   174

21. How Can We Release Life to the Lord?   178

    Bibliography   185

Acknowledgments

I am writing this book in collaboration with my friend Gregory Mira. Like I did, Gregory grew up in an atmosphere of serious prayer. He and his wife, Denise, have five sons, each of whom serve the Lord. Denise speaks at large conferences on raising children, and Gregory has ministered in many nations and also spoken at large conferences. He is no novice, and his thoughts are included in this effort.

Special thanks go to Mr. and Mrs. Michael Coleman, Dr. and Mrs. Ray Hester, Mr. and Mrs. Erik Krueger, Mr. and Mrs. Gene Hargis, Mr. and Mrs. Herman Kanis and all who have supported our publishing efforts through CSM Publishing.

I also am deeply grateful to the staff of Charles Simpson Ministries, who helped make this book a reality: Stephen Simpson, Susanne Simpson, Victoria Grace Simpson and Christina Villalobos.

Thank you to those at Chosen Books for the privilege of publishing with them. I am grateful to editorial director Jane Campbell and copy editor Catherine Cooker, who have made this a better book and have hopefully helped me become a better author.

1

What Is Prayer?

Honesty is the best policy—that is especially true of prayer, given that God knows us better than we know ourselves. Therefore, I will make every effort to be honest, for I am, like you, simply seeking to pray more effectively.

You are reading this because you believe, as I do, that prayer is a vital part of life; therefore, the questions and answers in this book are vital as well. If what we pray about is important, then how and why we pray will also be important.

A Foundation in Prayer

To introduce myself and my beliefs, I will share some of my story. Hopefully this will help you understand the answers that I offer to these questions about prayer.

My parents were "faith missionaries" in south Louisiana bayou country, ministering among French-speaking Catholics during the Great Depression. "Faith missionaries" meant we had no visible means of support—no salary. What support we had came from a small number of friends who, in that era, also had few resources. Fishing, hunting and gardening were not hobbies for us; they were survival skills.

Mother came from one of these French-speaking Catholic families. She met my father while he was ministering to people living along the bayous and swamps. He baptized most of her family in a cold, muddy canal one December, and then he began to minister in their home and to nearby relatives. In that era evangelicals found the going tough there—support was meager and opposition was plentiful.

Dad was from a small town in Alabama. When the Great Depression hit, my grandfather lost everything, and Dad had to drop out of college. He moved to New Orleans to get a job, and there he attended seminary. It was through a local Baptist church in New Orleans that Dad became interested in the bayous and doing mission work there.

I was born in 1937, during the heart of the Great Depression, in the south Louisiana bayous. My earliest memories took place in a homemade house trailer without indoor plumbing, running water or electricity. Looking back I see we were poor in money, yet we were rich in faith, courage and family. And we *did* have support from an occasional letter or a kind Catholic friend.

That was the context that imprinted my young consciousness; it is also how I learned about prayer. I heard my parents pray not only for food on the table but for friends and relatives to know Jesus Christ as Lord and Savior.

Sometimes we journeyed up the gravel road toward Kraemer, a small village along Bayou Boeuf, to Uncle Nory's house, where Dad held house meetings. The kids sat or lay on pallets while the singing, praying and teaching went on into the night. There was much to pray about. I was usually asleep by the time the meeting ended.

My parents often wept when they prayed because the subjects of their prayers were serious. Yet their prayers were effective: Churches were founded and people met the Lord, often in remote places like Grand Bayou, near the Mississippi River, where an entire village came to Christ.

Some time later my parents moved to south Alabama, where Dad pastored a Southern Baptist church, and their prayer life went with them. Upon retiring 35 years later, they came to work with me in the church that I pastored. Mom went home to be with the Lord in 1991, Dad in 1997. To their children and grandchildren they left a legacy of faith, prayer and the knowledge that God rewards those who diligently seek Him (see Hebrews 11:6). That is one legacy I aspire to leave as well.

The needs of our society are different now than they were for my parents in the bayous of the 1930s. We may have plumbing, electricity and numerous other conveniences, but the problems we face are sometimes more concerning: fractured families, moral confusion, a secular culture growing in hostility toward biblical values, intense polarization and other factors that strain our lives. We have not only an urgency to pray but an urgency to pray effectively.

Why were my parents' prayers effective? Why are some prayers answered and others are not? These are significant questions, and I will try to answer them, though I acknowledge that some answers await us in eternity. Scripture does, however, offer guidance that is available to us *now*, and we can also learn from our experiences as we grow in our relationships with Jesus.

My parents practiced prayer that was much more than mere discipline, a sign of "spirituality" or a means to get the Lord to do something. Prayer was the passionate pursuit of God and His will—it was survival and becoming more than conquerors in life's tests. It was about their children and others knowing God's will as well.

Their life of prayer bore fruit in my own family, as I practiced the lessons I learned from them with all three of my children. Each of them is in God's service today: Our older son, Stephen, is also a pastor. He says that all preachers' kids need therapy. I agree, and the Lord is a great therapist.

Our daughter, Charlyn, is a missionary with her husband, Enrique. Jonathan, our younger son, works with me in publishing. He learned by watching his older siblings. My dear wife and partner in the Gospel, Carolyn, has been with the Lord since 2008 (I will share more about her later).

Given to God

Let me give one very significant example of the effect my parents' prayers had on my life. At the age of seventeen, despite the fact that I was not walking with the Lord, I feared that the Lord might call me to become a minister. It was the last thing I wanted to do with my life. One Saturday night I wandered in late, as usual. My father and mother did not go to sleep until I came in. This wayward behavior was a great concern, not to mention a terrible inconvenience, as Sunday morning would come early and my Dad would preach on a short night's rest.

On this typical Saturday night, I arrived to find my father at the door, looking very serious. "Charles, you know what your mother and I did tonight?"

"No, sir."

"We gave you to God. God gave you to us, and we don't know what to do with you, so we gave you back."

That scared me. For all of my bravado and rebellion, I feared God. From then on my parents took a hands-off approach to my life, but God took a hands-on approach. I learned that God is God and I am not. The Lord "scared the devil out of me," as incident after incident convinced me that I was no longer dealing with Dad and Mom—I was dealing with the Almighty!

Months later I knew beyond a doubt that God was not just calling me, He was "threatening" me. I once heard Billy Graham

16

say, "Fear may not be the best motive, but it beats no motive at all." Yes, the Lord loves us, but sometimes He loves us enough to do whatever is necessary to save us from ourselves.

The stories of God's dealing with me are too numerous to tell here, but one remarkable example came on a night I was car racing a friend and got lost. Thinking the road went straight, I came unexpectedly to a ninety-degree curve; I tried to take it to avoid the ditch beyond, and the car lifted onto two wheels. I could have struck a match on the pavement. Had the car flipped, this book would never have been written. It seemed to stay that way forever. (My friend, who was behind me, told me, "I saw the whole underside of your car!") Then I heard the Lord say, "How would you like to be a minister?"

Finally I met with my father, admitting, "Dad, I think that the Lord is calling me to preach." It was tough to even say it, given that I knew myself, church life and some of the demands placed on ministers. I knew also from experience that money would be tight. Dad and Mom never laid any of that on my shoulders, but I knew it.

"Charles, you need to know something that we never told you before: When you were born, we gave you to God. We prayed over you and dedicated you to Him." So now I had been given to God twice: once at birth, then again at seventeen (thanks, Dad). Then he and I prayed together in tears, knowing that it would not be easy—but that if it was the will of God, He would see me through, for He is faithful. I was right about one thing: Given my nature, it would not be easy for me.

The Rewarder

Hebrews 11:6 tells us that God is a rewarder of those who diligently seek Him. There are three very important words in that phrase: *seek, diligently* and *reward*. While this is not a formula, it does offer a solid model. We get out of prayer what we put in. Diligent seeking is not casual, perfunctory or mere routine. If the rewards are significant, then so must be the effort of the heart. Drawing near to God with our words only is distasteful to Him and fails to bring the rewards of diligently seeking Him (see Isaiah 29:13).

Dad often reminded me of the great prayer warriors of yesteryear, who changed the world around them through their earnest prayers: "Praying Hyde," Adoniram Judson, Andrew Murray and a host of others. Now is our time to turn the tide, but it will take a fresh look at those who were effective, both in the Bible and in subsequent history, in order to succeed.

So my purpose in writing this book is to help us pray more biblically and effectively, as well as reap the promised rewards of those kinds of prayers. The issues facing us in this world are urgent and daunting; only God can save us and our offspring. We do not have time to waste on meaninglessness if we are to take advantage of the lessons passed on by our forefathers.

Recently I encountered a young friend who was working as a clerk. Looking more distraught than I had seen him before, he told me his dad had had a stroke. "Do you believe in prayer?" I asked. "I wish I believed more," he responded. I took his hand and prayed.

This man represents millions who, like him, carry a great burden and wish they could believe more—this is especially true of the young, and maybe true of you and me. I want him and all of us to believe more and reap more of the promised rewards through effective prayer.

What Is Effective Prayer?

The person who thinks that he or she has a perfect comprehension of prayer is hindered from the very beginning (see Isaiah

55:8–9). We begin our prayer journey with humility. I will describe (not define) prayer as *the sincere expression of our heart's desire to God*. Sometimes it is a thought; other times it is a verbal expression that takes a lot of time and soul-searching. It can even be agonizing if the issues are serious and buried deep inside. The good news is that the Lord wants to hear us and is willing to help us—if we ask.

This book will often refer to the Holy Spirit, just as the Bible does, because He is here to help us pray, to know our real desires and to express them. The Holy Spirit is God's own Spirit, who has come alongside us to teach and guide us in the process (see John 14–16; Romans 8:26). He is also here to help us know the will of God, the primary purpose of prayer.

Elijah is a great example of an effective man of prayer. James 5:13–20 speaks about Elijah's type of effective prayer: how it alleviates suffering, heals the sick, brings forgiveness of sins, brings rain and turns sinners from the error of their ways. Those are all great rewards! This passage also tells us to confess our trespasses and pray fervently.

First Kings 17–18 describe the events surrounding Elijah's prayers: It was a dark time for Israel, whose people had turned from God to worship the idols Baal and Asherah, god and goddess of fertility. Elijah confronted King Ahab about the wickedness of his reign, for Ahab had previously killed the righteous Naboth and stolen his vineyard. When Elijah prayed, the rain stopped for three and a half years. One can only imagine what devastation such a draught would cause for the economy of an agrarian nation. At God's command Elijah left Israel and went to Sidon.

After three and a half years, Elijah returned to challenge the prophets of Baal and Asherah to a contest on Mount Carmel, overlooking the Mediterranean Sea near present-day Haifa. The contest would determine whose prayers would be answered, and lives were at stake. As thousands watched, the false prophets prayed profusely and desperately, cutting themselves and prophesying until the evening. No one answered.

Finally Elijah repaired the neglected altar of God and prayed simply, using few words. Fire fell from heaven. Then the rain came. The people fell on their faces and cried, "The LORD, He is God! The LORD, He is God!" (1 Kings 18:39).

Elijah was effective. This is the model that James offers us for repentance, forgiveness, healing, turning sinners from the error of their ways and even bringing fire and rain.

Jesus also gave us an example of two men who prayed: One was effective, the other was not (Luke 18:9–14). This parable is a glimpse into how the Lord responds to prayer. The religious man boasted in his own good works and thanked God that he was not like the despised tax collector. The tax collector was so aware of his own failures that he could not even lift his eyes to pray. He just stood with head bowed, and striking his chest he cried out, "God, be merciful to me a sinner!" (verse 13).

The Lord concluded that the religious man was just talking to himself. It was the tax collector who went home justified. Amazing. One man was arrogant, condescending and not heard by the Lord. The other was humble and begged for the mercy of God—he was "justified." That is an important word. My friend Derek Prince used to say that *justified* means "just-as-if-I'd never sinned." The unrighteous man was counted righteous because he saw his own problem, humbled himself and cast himself on God's mercy.

Apparently God hates pride but loves humility and faith. The latter is the basis for justification, or how God sees us. It was this discovery that changed the course of modern history, as Martin Luther and others came to understand Scriptures like Habakkuk 2:4 and Romans 1:17, believing that the just shall live by faith. We do not earn credits with God, though

He will bless right behavior; we are counted righteous through faith and obedience. This fundamental truth is foundational to our prayers. We begin from the heart, in humility and faith in the One to whom we speak. That positions us to receive God's goodness and mercy—both are gifts. When prayers come from our hearts, they will touch God's heart. Such prayers can change our lives and affect the issues we are praying about.

In the next chapter we will look at the greatest of all mysteries, God Himself, the Creator of all that exists. In prayer we are entering into a different realm—beyond our natural comprehension, invisible, infinite, eternal—to approach the living God. We do not really know how to pray as we should, but the Lord has given His divine Holy Spirit to help us (see John 14:26; 16:13–15). He wants to show us the path into the very presence of God. Who are we talking to when we pray? Let us examine that question in order to build our faith and grow in prayer.

Discussion Questions

1. Why is prayer a mystery? What does prayer mean to you?

2. Have you been born again?

3. What does it mean to come boldly to the throne of grace?

4. Have you ever prayed with someone to receive Jesus as Lord and Savior?

5. Do you have a prayer list?

6. How would you describe effective praying?

7. What was the difference between the very religious man and the tax collector? Have you ever been one or both of these men?

8. Is prayer a priority in your daily life?

2

Who Am I Talking to Here?

Each day before I pray, I ask myself, "Who am I about to talk to?" I try to meditate on who God is—His attributes, His words, His involvement in the lives of humans—and realize that *this* is the One to whom I am about to speak, and hopefully the One I will hear.

A favorite song of mine was written by my friend Pete Sanchez: "I Exalt Thee."

> For Thou, O Lord, art high above all the earth.
> Thou art exalted far above all gods.
> I exalt Thee, O Lord!

One of the tragedies of modern culture and failed prayer is the casual use of the name of God. In the Ten Commandments we are instructed not to take the name of the Lord our God in vain, or in an empty, disrespectful manner. In fact, the first four Commandments are about honoring God. When they fail to honor God, people lose an understanding of who God is. We should approach Him with a desire to know Him and His will. He is who He is, and we are not.

My experience is that as children, we usually think of God as the one to ask for things that we desire. But as we grow older, we should begin to consider who He is and what He wants. This is what David did while he tended sheep in the fields and gazed at the night skies. His thoughts on creation began shaping his view of God, the world and his own life.

The Creator

Out of those observations and meditations came Psalm 8:

> O LORD, our Lord, how excellent is Your name in all the earth, who have set Your glory above the heavens! . . . When I consider Your heavens, the work of Your fingers, the moon and the stars, which You have ordained, what is man that You are mindful of him, and the son of man that You visit him? For You have made him a little lower than the angels, and You have crowned him with glory and honor. You have made him to have dominion over the works of Your hands; You have put all things under his feet.
>
> Psalm 8:1, 3–6

David was awed by what he saw and awed by the One who made it. The problem some people have is that when they discover something, they act as though they created it. Not so with David—the wonder of creation led him to humility and worship.

One evening my wife, Carolyn, and I sat at the ocean's edge on Grand Cayman Island and gazed at the stars. I had never seen so many—millions of them. Living in and around cities robs us of such a view. It was like a glittering canopy that fell into the distant waters; it took our breath away. It must have been like what David saw.

Some scientists estimate that there are one hundred fifty billion galaxies, each containing millions of stars, and that galaxies are still being created. Surely our God is an awesome God. The amazing thing is that not only did He create all of that and more, but this same God visits *us*. We can talk and listen to Him. How renewing and life-giving!

How we view creation and how we view God will shape our worldview, our view of ourselves and our prayer life. It will affect everything that we think and do, the height of our faith and the depth of our love and gratitude. This Creator of all that exists is holy (see Colossians 1:16–18; 3:1–4); human arrogance in the face of creation is sheer folly.

God's Ways

Perhaps the most telling fact about creation is its consistency from the smallest scale to the largest. Creation is not random or chaotic but consistent. Without consistent creation principles and fixed natural laws, there could be no math, science, seasons or predictable outcomes. When we learn those natural laws and apply them, there are rewards and blessings to be received.

So it is in the spiritual world, which was created by God along with the natural world. This is not a sign that He has a multiple personality disorder; rather truth proceeds from one Source in both the natural and spiritual worlds. Though His ways and thoughts are higher than ours in the same way the heavens are higher than the earth, God does have ways that we can learn as we study His Word and grow in fellowship (see 1 Kings 3:14; Psalm 103:7). Learning God's ways pays great dividends, just as learning natural laws does. Progress in any area depends on following a particular way, but many refuse to accept God, hoping to find some other source, another way.

Jesus said, "I am the way, the truth, and the life. No one comes to the Father except through Me" (John 14:6). It is amazing that many would accept the reality of space aliens but deny their own Creator (see John 1:11). Some of these are not people of low IQ. Romans 1:18–22 tells of the tragic results of excluding God from our knowledge: "Professing to be wise, they became fools." Could that happen to an entire nation? We need look no further than the French, Nazi and Bolshevik revolutions; they were horrific slaughters led by atheists, smart people who acted as fools.

His Presence

On the other hand, when we acknowledge God and His presence, amazing things happen. One of my more striking memories of corporate prayer is of a time years ago when a prayer partner and I met each Saturday for prayer, sometimes lasting through much of the night. We had agreed not to discuss our prayer time with others or invite others to join unless we both concurred, because harmony in our prayer time was of utmost importance.

One Saturday evening, I arrived at our place of prayer to find a man sitting in a wheelchair, waiting. I assumed that my friend had invited him, though he had not.

"Have you come here for prayer?" I asked.

"Yes, I have," he replied.

We exchanged small talk, but my prayer partner did not arrive. I decided that though my friend was detained, we should go ahead and begin to pray. I had scarcely gotten on my knees when the other man began a prayer that lasted, it seemed, for 45 minutes.

I call that particular type of prayer "preaching to Jesus," not for its duration but for its content. He seemed to be informing

God, and perhaps me, of his religious knowledge. During his prolonged prayer, my friend quietly slipped in. My friend and I normally waited on the Lord until we sensed His presence; this other brother "took over" immediately. I do not think the Lord minded because He had not yet "arrived" either! After a while the prayer ceased, and now the three of us were quiet for several minutes.

I do not understand the presence of God, but on some occasions it manifests in a very evident way. The atmosphere changes, sometimes suddenly, as it did that evening. You could almost feel the breeze as the Holy Spirit came in, the same Spirit that hovered over the waters in Genesis 1. At the same instant the man fell from the wheelchair, face planted on the floor. It was startling, but not nearly as startling as what happened next. He began another long prayer, this one quite different. I think that he confessed every sin he had ever committed. My friend and I were both embarrassed and wanted to let him be alone with God, but we were afraid to move or open our mouths for fear that we might be next.

It was as though God had him by the rib cage and was squeezing the sin out of him. He was confessing, groaning, weeping, confessing some more. It took what seemed an interminably long time. When he had finally finished, he climbed back into the wheelchair and apologized, not for his confessions, but for his previous prayer and his insensitivity to the Holy Spirit. We were not about to be critical—just amazed and awed by the power and presence of God.

Who Is Present?

Who is this God we call "Father"? The writers of the Old Covenant would not even write His name. He was referred to as all of the following:

26

- Lord
- El Roi—the God who sees me
- YHWH—I am or the One who is
- Elohim—the God of might
- Jehovah Shammah—the God who is present
- Jehovah Rapha—the Lord our healer
- Jehovah Tsidkenu—the Lord our righteousness
- Jehovah Jireh—the Lord our provider
- Jehovah Nissi—the Lord our banner
- Jehovah Shalom—the Lord our peace
- Lord Sabbaoth—the Lord of armies (hosts)
- Jehovah Gmolah—the God of recompense
- El Elyon—the most high God
- El Shaddai—God almighty
- El Olam—the everlasting God

and numerous other names that reveal His Sovereign character and power.

Then there are the names of Jesus: the Word of God, the Faithful and True, the First and the Last, Captain of the Lord's host. We know Him as Jesus, "Jehovah saves." He is God made flesh, who dwells among us, full of grace and truth. He is "the One who is and who was and who is to come" (Revelation 11:17). He is the same yesterday, today and forever (see Hebrews 13:8).

When the presence comes, this is who is present with us. He is Immanuel, "God with us."

Is it any wonder that this God said to Jeremiah, "Call to Me, and I will answer you, and show you great and mighty things, which you do not know" (Jeremiah 33:3). It was this God who asked Jeremiah, "Is anything too hard for Me?" This is the One who was revealed in the Christ: who walked on water, cast out evil spirits, healed the sick, turned water into wine and fed thousands with five loaves and two fish. This is the One who raised the dead and was Himself raised from the dead. When we pray, we are talking to this God through Jesus Christ, who ever lives to make intercession for us (see Hebrews 7:25).

Pride, secular philosophy, sin, distraction and a host of other issues have robbed us of our fellowship with the God of the Bible and the rewards of diligently seeking Him. Often they have robbed us of our loved ones, children, righteousness, joy and peace—the very Kingdom of God. They have robbed our finances and our future. It is time to plunder the kingdom of darkness and reclaim our blessings through prayer—and we can, if we realize who we are talking to when we pray. Nothing, absolutely nothing, is impossible with God (see Luke 1:37).

Jesus was serious while on earth, and He is serious now. Yes, He rejoiced and had fellowship with others, but His purpose was ever before Him. He saw the awful calamity that was coming for Israel, and He understood that mankind needed a Savior. He was serious enough to endure the crucifixion for us. It is time for His people to become just as serious about prayer. Later we will look more closely at Jesus' prayer life, but first let us examine reasons to pray, as we consider why we should be serious about prayer in the next chapter.

Discussion Questions

1. Why should you meditate on God before hurrying through your prayer?

2. What kind of hymns are your favorites? Do words matter?

3. What is your foundation for faith in God? What is the strongest evidence of His existence?

4. What keeps us from acknowledging God and being thankful?

5. Why is the consistency of natural law important to our lives?

6. What does "the manifest presence of God" mean to you?

7. What are some names of God? And Jesus?

8. What would it look like if we became more serious about God?

3

Why Pray?

The year was 1787, and representatives from the individual American states gathered in Philadelphia to form a new constitution. In some ways the United States were not so unified. The Articles of Confederation, which had governed the nation since 1777, proved weak and ineffective. There was still discord among the former colonies, much of it religious in nature.

Each state followed its own predominate version of Christianity, while some individuals were deists. The Anglicans in Virginia were considered suspect due to their ties with England. The Baptists of Rhode Island did not trust the government to protect religious freedom. The Catholics of Maryland were viewed as papists governed by Rome. The Congregationalists of New England viewed central authority as dangerous, while the Quakers of Pennsylvania were opposed to war. Needless to say, the various Christian and political leaders did not pray together.

Prior to the Declaration of Independence, in the mid-1700s, a spiritual revival called the "Great Awakening" swept the colonies. Men like Jonathan Edwards and George Whitefield were instrumental in bringing the Gospel to many of the two and a half million residents. It was estimated that Whitefield preached to half of the total population, and much of his preaching occurred outdoors. He also became a friend to Benjamin Franklin, who attended Whitefield's meetings in Philadelphia and hosted him in his own home. Franklin estimated some crowds to be larger than twenty thousand people. Whitefield's meetings often brought people from different brands of Christianity together in the streets to hear the Gospel and to pray.[1]

When the Constitutional Convention gathered in Philadelphia in 1787, the various representatives faced great dissension because many were unsettled about a stronger central government. It was Benjamin Franklin who suggested each session begin with prayer, quoting from Daniel 4:25, which says that God rules in the affairs of men. The delegates did pray together; some, for the first time ever, prayed with those of different views. The Lord answered their prayers and assisted them in establishing our Constitution, based on the philosophies of Christian thinkers in Europe such as Locke, Blackstone and Sidney.

After the Constitution was approved and the Bill of Rights added, Franklin was asked, "What kind of government have you given us?"

His answer was, "A Republic, if you can keep it."[2]

Keeping the Republic

And how can we keep it? By following the instructions of the apostle Paul:

1. Arnold A. Dallimore, *George Whitefield: The Life and Times of the Great Evangelist of the Eighteenth-Century Revival, Volume I*, 2d ed. (Westchester, Ill.: Cornerstone Books, 1980), 296.

2. Matthew Spalding, *We Still Hold These Truths* (Wilmington, Del.: Intercollegiate Studies Institute, 2011), 3.

> Therefore I exhort first of all that supplications, prayers, interces-
> sions, and giving of thanks be made for all men, for kings and
> all who are in authority, that we may lead a quiet and peaceable
> life in all godliness and reverence. For this is good and acceptable
> in the sight of God our Savior.
>
> 1 Timothy 2:1–3

Since our nation was founded in revival and prayer, the only
way to preserve it is by the same means. At his inauguration,
George Washington, the United States' first president (from
1789 to 1797), led government officials into St. Paul's Chapel in
New York City to dedicate our nation to God. New York was
the first capital of the United States, and this was the government's first official act. It should be noted that the Twin Towers
of the World Trade Center, which were destroyed on September
11, 2001, stood on St. Paul's Chapel property, sacred soil. One
miracle of 9/11 was that St. Paul's was not damaged, but that
is another story.[3]

Washington called on the Lord in his farewell address, warning against division, encroachment of one branch of government
over another, losing our morality and the problems of debt and
foreign entanglements (particularly with nations of Europe).[4]
Washington was more than a president, he was a prophet.

Wake Up!

Because the Lord has offered His people the rewards of effective
prayer, should we not accept a large measure of responsibility for
the condition of our beloved nation? Many Christians neither

3. Lyndon Harris, "Sanctuary at Ground Zero," *National Geographic Magazine*, http://ngm.nationalgeographic.com/ngm/0209/st_pauls/online_extra.html,
accessed April 3, 2013.

4. George Washington, "Farewell Address" (1796), Lillian Goldman Law Library, http://avalon.law.yale.edu/18th_century/washing.asp.

seriously pray for our nation nor vote, and they are entangled in lesser issues. Again, as the apostle Paul said, "It is high time to awake out of sleep" (Romans 13:11). Prayer should be our priority! Let's start with all those in authority, so that we can lead a "peaceable life in all godliness and reverence."

Another very significant reason to pray is for our children and the youth of our nation, who are being taught secularism and are dropping out of church life at an alarming rate. Scripture stresses the importance of not neglecting children; over and over we are instructed to train our children, as did Noah and Abraham after him (see Genesis 18:19). Psalm 78:6 tells us to pass on our history to our children and their children, and Proverbs 22:6 says, "Train up a child in the way he should go, and when he is old he will not depart from it." The Ten Commandments teach God first and family next. In the New Testament, we see Jesus relating to children (see Matthew 19:14) and are reminded by Paul to train our children (see Ephesians 6:1–4). Too often our children have been lost while we have pursued lesser things; as a result, they have never seen the power of God.

The Necessity of Training

Once, when our children were young, we went out to eat at a restaurant, and they behaved well. A lady at the next table said, "I wish my children behaved like yours." We were flattered, though we knew that our children did not do so always. But Carolyn and I understood that a child's behavior requires more than wishing; it requires consistent, fervent prayer and painful discipline—often more painful to the parent than the child.

The saying goes, "The family that prays together, stays together." What is the state of marriage and family telling us about family prayer? The divorce rate climbs, even among Christians, with the accompanying problems for children. What God has joined together, we have put asunder, and then we lament the state of our nation's moral climate. Many of our children are "parented" by peers, celebrities and the media. In the process we have aborted over fifty million unwanted children, a legacy that continues to haunt us.

Nearly every day I receive a letter requesting prayer for children or grandchildren. I join those requests and try to answer each one. The real answer is praying both for and with our children from birth, allowing them to see firsthand the power of prayer in their lives before they go out into a hostile moral environment and secular education.

I remember my brushes with this kind of education. My introductory course in college geology was taught by a professor who was an atheist and swore in class. He freely ridiculed faith, the theology of creation and other convictions I held. To challenge him meant risking a lower grade, and most of the large class sat in silence, while others accepted his views. The large majority of freshmen were, sadly, affected and lost much of their moral foundation.

Then there was Introduction to Philosophy. The professor was an affable ordained minister in a prominent denomination. He had a drinking problem, however, and he also had a wreck—he ran into a cow. We joked that we did not know if the cow was in the road or the professor was in the pasture.

The Benefit

Thank God I was prepared by praying parents to face college and later seminary. Many, if not most, young people are not so blessed, and their "education" becomes a dismantling of faith, with cynicism as the consequence. With that foundation, their lives, marriages (if they marry) and vocations become something much less than the rewards offered by God.

My parents prayed for and with me, and that has had lasting benefits in my life. I remember an occasion when Dad and I were praying together after I had professed my personal faith in Jesus. I always began my prayers with "Dear God . . ." After we concluded our prayers, Dad said to me, "You do not need to say, 'Dear God,' any longer; you can say, 'Dear Father,' because God *is* your Father in heaven." I will never forget his words that evening. God is my Father! (Unlike many young people, I had good associations with the word *Father*.) I knew my Father went to college with me in a very real way.

Another occasion for prayer came a little later. In 1957 I gave up on dating. Sure, there were lots of good Christian women in the schools that I attended, but I came to realize that becoming a minister would put an extra burden on my decision. Dad had married a woman of exceptional character and a gentle and quiet spirit, and she became a great mother. I had also known of ministers who had been limited by their marriage choices. Given both my temperament and calling to be a minister, I knew that my decision regarding marriage called for prayer—serious prayer. So I often asked the Lord, who knew me, my needs and His own will, to guide me in my choice.

I often commuted a hundred miles from my home to the college that I attended and would frequently ride with friends. One of them regularly mentioned a young woman that he knew. He may have been trying to set us up for a date, but it was obvious that he also had a high regard for her. I was twenty years old and pastoring a church, and I told this friend that the church needed someone to play piano for a special series of meetings. He answered, "She plays piano too."

So I came by her house and met her watchful mother. This young woman was not only beautiful but had great character and a quiet spirit (desirable qualities in a wife, according to 1 Peter 3:1–4), like my own mother. Her parents were committed

Christians, as were my own. In fact, our fathers had roomed together for one year while at college, though we had not known it; we had never met before. I asked if she would play piano for those meetings, and she agreed. After she played for the meetings, we began a fifty-year relationship that I am convinced came from prayer.

The great decisions of life are usually made when we are young, but the results are reaped later in life. Marriage, faith and vocation are three important decisions that we cannot afford to make without seeking God, who knows the end from the beginning. Many people miss the rewards of a happy marriage because they neglect to pray. Or they get into the wrong vocation or embark on a path without God. Prayer is more important in youth than at any other time (see Ecclesiastes 12:1). Life is not a practice run; you only get to do it once.

The Great Commission

Praying for leaders, family, vocation and children is important and necessary, but we must not neglect the Great Commission:

> And Jesus came and spoke to them, saying, "All authority has been given to Me in heaven and on earth. Go therefore and make disciples of all the nations, baptizing them in the name of the Father and of the Son and of the Holy Spirit, teaching them to observe all things that I have commanded you; and lo, I am with you always, even to the end of the age."
>
> Matthew 28:18–20

I have discovered that among Christians, making disciples is, strangely, a highly controversial subject. It is something that we began to think belonged to international missionaries, and while many of them have done it well, what about the people right where we live? The world begins at our front door.

Unfortunately, many people forget this. I have been surprised many times by how people respond when I ask, "How many of you have a prayer list that includes several non-Christians?" Too many Christians pray primarily about their own needs to the exclusion of those who need Jesus. Yet we call Him "Lord" and His command "the Great Commission." We teach and learn a lot about having faith for our needs—and wants—but what are we learning about faith for those who need Jesus, whose natural and eternal lives are in jeopardy?

Several years ago I went to Novosibirsk, the principal city in Siberia, to visit a thriving church of more than two thousand people in a most difficult environment. The pastor had faithfully preached the Gospel, baptized and made disciples. That morning as I spoke, several people came to Christ, one of them an eighty-year-old woman. Since that time, the pastor has moved to Ukraine to start another church, and he continues to make new disciples.

Discipling is a prayer priority for those who minister and labor in the harshest of circumstances, such as China, the Middle East and Sudan. I recently met a Sudanese minister who was making disciples. As he told me of the suffering and persecution there, I felt humbled by his devotion.

Pray About Everything

In addition to praying for leaders, family and making disciples, we should pray about anything that concerns us. Our Father in heaven cares about the totality of our lives. But self-concerns should come after His concerns. Prayer is not so much about *informing God* as it is about *getting in tune with God*. What are His concerns for the world, the Church and my (or your) personal direction? What is His will on earth? This is our primary concern, and after this come prayers for daily bread, personal forgiveness, avoiding temptation and being delivered from the evil one (see Matthew 6:9–13).

We are told to pray about many things: the peace of Jerusalem (Psalm 122:6), the peace of our homes and cities (Jeremiah 29:7), on behalf of those who spitefully use us (Matthew 5:44) and for laborers and the harvest (Matthew 9:38). We are also invited to pray for things that we desire (John 15:16); for those who come to faith after we are gone (John 17:20); for the unity of the Church (John 17:21); for the sanctification of our spirit, soul and body (1 Thessalonians 5:23); for healing (James 5:13–14) and for deliverance from evil spirits (Matthew 17:21). It is safe to say that we should pray about all of our cares and desires because He cares for us; He is our Father. He wants to give good gifts to us (see Matthew 7:11).

Many years ago, one of my parishioners advised another, "Don't tell Brother Charles; all he'll say is 'Pray about it!'" While that was not exactly true, I do believe that if more people prayed first, there would be less need for counseling. Jesus is the Wonderful Counselor, the Prince of Peace. *We expect too much from others and not enough from God.*

My life verse is Psalm 126:5–6: "Those who sow in tears shall reap in joy. He who continually goes forth weeping, bearing seed for sowing, shall doubtless come again with rejoicing, bringing his sheaves with him." The best way to improve your life is to improve your prayer life. My greatest joys were the result of prayer, while my greatest sorrows were the result of failing to pray. Prayer can save us from many things, but most importantly, it can save us from ourselves (see James 4:1–10).

The rewards of prayer are innumerable: the power of the Holy Spirit, good leaders, good families, godly children, disciples, met needs, a peaceful life, success in our endeavors, overcoming life-destroying temptations, wise decisions, deliverance from evil and evil spirits and usefulness to the almighty Father. Those are life's greatest rewards!

We are assured in 2 Corinthians 1:20 that "all the promises of God in Him are Yes, and in Him Amen, to the glory of God through us." So I am praying to demonstrate to others that God is faithful and that His promises are true. I am securing the rewards of God's goodness and mercy for our land, my family, my disciples and my life—all for His glory.

In the next chapter we will look at Jesus' prayer life and how He prayed, learning from Him how to pray more effectively.

Discussion Questions

1. What are the major issues about which you pray?

2. How do your heart and motive matter to God?

3. How did prayer affect the founding of our nation?

4. How does prayer affect your family? Your city?

5. In what ways has this chapter affected your prayer life?

6. Do you believe that the Lord answers all prayers? If not, why?

7. Can you cite an example of a prayer in the New Testament that was rejected?

8. Name three priorities for prayer.

4

What Can I Learn from Jesus' Prayers?

My dad used to say, "I wouldn't take a million dollars for that experience . . . but I would not give a nickel for another one like it." The year 1965 gave me that same feeling.

The year before, 1964, was a memorable year filled with joy and wonderful outcomes. Seven years earlier, at the age of twenty, I had started pastoring a church in Mobile, Alabama. Yes, that is too young! The church called me anyway because their situation was so desperate—attendance was down to 35 people, and the church could barely pay the interest on its loans. I had been preaching for about a year and a half while at college in Birmingham, so someone recommended me for the task. After serving as an interim pastor for several months, they invited me to pastor full-time. I was inexpensive.

I began commuting a hundred miles to another college for my junior and senior years, and in the meantime, the church grew. After graduating I commuted one hundred fifty miles to seminary in New Orleans; the church continued to grow. But I did not take well to seminary; I was a "fundamentalist" with a very literal approach to the Bible and resisted neoorthodoxy and liberalism. Commuting, stress, studying Greek and Hebrew and other issues took a toll on me, and in 1962 I had all the symptoms of a heart attack at age 26. Perhaps it was simply a panic attack, but another ministerial student in my New Testament class actually died. He was also a pastor and commuter. Months later I quit seminary for the second and final time.

I decided to throw myself into just building the church with hard work and Bible preaching; it seemed to go well since we were now up to three hundred people. My fellow pastors elected me secretary of the local association, which had ninety churches, and this was a great honor. I was a member of a local country club, where I played golf. I was becoming "well-thought-of"—a precarious perch.

"I Want to Go There"

Now, as I turned my focus to church, Bible study and witnessing to others, something was happening inside of me. I began comparing the early Church to our church—how they prayed, gave finances and saw both the power of God and people coming to Christ. I hungered for all of it, but I felt empty; I was burned out at only 27 years of age. Looking at myself and the church made me think of the old spiritual: "Not my brother or my sister, but it's me, oh Lord, standing in the need of prayer." I saw a church mostly full of seemingly empty people, and the Lord was saying, *If you had anything to give them, you would have done so by now.* Someone had said, "If you want a revival, then draw a circle, get in it, and pray until revival comes in the circle." That spoke to me. It grieves a Bible believer to see how far the Church has fallen; sadder still, I was part of the process. I had bonded to success, but not so much to the voice of God.

That is where I was when I heard that my friend Ken Sumrall, who was the senior pastor of Boulevard Baptist Church in Pensacola, had had an experience with the Holy Spirit. His church, which had nine hundred members, subsequently fired him over it. Then he began a small church in a storefront. In spite of the disgrace that surrounds being fired, I drove to Pensacola to attend Ken's prayer meeting; I left five hours later feeling as though the meeting had been much shorter than five hours. The presence of God was palpable. The next week I drove back, seeking the same presence. While I was reading Romans 14:17 ("For the kingdom of God is not eating and drinking, but righteousness and peace and joy in the Holy Spirit"), the presence of the Holy Spirit came upon me like a flood! I laughed and wept simultaneously. The joy, peace and righteousness had been missing, but it all seemed to come with the Holy Spirit. That was April 1964.

Just two months earlier, we had had a "revival" in our church that revived no one, including me. Though the preaching and worship seemed good, nothing happened. If I had said, "If you love your mother, come forward," no one would have moved. God had dried up the river; our baptistery had cobwebs.

But now heaven had come down, and I had a personal revival. The first Sunday after my experience in the Holy Spirit, heaven came down in our church, too. About fifty people came to the altar even before I invited them, many with tears of repentance. Others stood, stunned. One lady with a mixture of tears and mascara running down her cheeks said, "I don't know where you have been, but I want to go there."

We broke all our records right through the summer: conversions, attendance, finances and every other thing we measured. It was a wonderful time, really "New Testament." Good things were happening—a pastor's dream. But other things were happening that I did not see at first. Some thought that I was too "Pentecostal," though there were no "manifestations" in our services. I was simply confronting the people with their condition and the claims of the Bible, but some did not appreciate what I was saying. They liked the way it had been before.

Tough Times

Finally, in the fall of 1964, one of our best deacons asked me, "Do you believe that the gifts of the Holy Spirit are for today?" I said that I did; I believed it all. He replied that it was not our denominational position. My response was that I had been called to preach the Bible—all of it. He soon left the church, along with others. He was a good man, a friend on the original committee that had invited me to become their pastor. I had baptized his children, his entire family had been part of our success and he rightly had influence in the church.

What a difference eight months made. In April, it was joy unspeakable; by Christmas, three hundred had shrunk to one hundred fifty. We had recently borrowed $100,000 and doubled the size of the auditorium. Now we had to rope off large sections; you could drive a truck through it and hit nobody. The finance chairman, who was vice president of our city's largest bank, would tell me, "I'll give you ninety more days—you'll be bankrupt!" He seemed to hope for just that. A once-popular minister was now a pariah, a heretic, a "Holy Roller." The church would vote on whether to keep me, and I would win by a large majority; but people still left, and I had lost thirty pounds by December. Those who left took their grievances with them to other churches, and our local church controversy spread throughout the area. Now what would we do?

My wife had married a young and successful pastor. Now some of those who left our church went to her parents' church, telling their stories to the very pastor who had performed our wedding ceremony. Carolyn's father was a deacon in that church, and though he and her mother were gracious, they no doubt wondered what was happening to me—and what would happen to Carolyn and our one-year-old son.

Needless to say, my prayer life deepened; the Lord had blessed me with a diligent and supportive prayer partner and others who were praying for the church and me. But Christmas did not look promising, and our personal finances, as well as the church's, were in jeopardy.

Out of Nowhere

Christmas was only a few days away when my phone rang.

"Is this Charles Simpson?" a woman asked.

"Yes, to whom am I speaking?"

"That is none of your business, but I want to do something for you" was the response.

I was curious. "You know that favors for me won't buy anything."

She pressed on. "Look, the Lord wants me to do something. Are you gonna let me do it?"

"Okay, what does the Lord want you do?"

"I want you to go to a certain furniture store and get some furniture that I picked out; I knew that being a preacher you would get the cheap stuff. This is *good* furniture, and there's some for your son's room too. Then go around the corner to the art shop and get some paintings that I picked out that match the furniture. Next week, someone will come by and measure for drapes."

I held the phone in stunned silence. It seemed like a dream, and it still does. We had almost no furniture, and what we did have was the "cheap stuff." *Curtains?* I thought. *Furniture for my son?* These things had been beyond our ability to buy. In today's money she gave at least $30,000 or $40,000 worth of furniture, drapes and art, but it was not the money that affected me. It was God's grace beyond even my faith.

She never would meet me or tell me who she was. I tried to witness to her by phone, but I do not know if she ever became a believer. I did find out years later that she ran a brothel. It is amazing the people God uses!

Jesus' Prayer Life

It was in those days that I studied the life of Jesus again, not for theology but for help in a time of trouble. I especially looked into His prayer life and even watched Him pray in my mind's eye. Here "the very God" talked to "the very God" in the divine Holy Spirit—amazing! Awesome! Do not let anyone tell you that they comprehend the Trinity; I am not about to try. It is simply holy.

In my difficult times I entered into His fellowship through prayer. As I envisioned Jesus in prayer—even as I struggled with His sovereign will in those dark days—I could see the heavens and was lifted out of my situation. That is the testimony of many who see Jesus, even in martyrdom (see Acts 7:54–60). My pain was light in comparison (see 2 Corinthians 4:16–18). My worst days became my best days in fellowship with my Lord. One of my very first sermons at the church had been from Philippians 3:7–16; now I was walking in it: "Forgetting those things which are behind . . . I press toward the goal for the prize" (verses 13–14).

I realized that if I humbled myself, He would lift me up—not easy, but necessary! If the Son of God could humble Himself to become one of us, die on the cross and sweat blood in the garden, who was I to resist humbling myself (see Philippians 2:5–11)? I could, by His amazing grace, fellowship with Jesus there in my valley as never before on my mountains. And it is to fellowship that He has called us! We cannot fellowship if we do not walk where He walked; after all, He said, "Follow Me."

How Jesus Prayed

So, let's look at where Jesus walked in His prayer life.

Luke 3:21–22—Jesus was baptized by John, and when He prayed, the Holy Spirit came upon Him. This gives insight into the connection between baptism, prayer and the Holy Spirit. *We can fellowship with Him in baptism, prayer and being filled with and led by the Holy Spirit.*

Mark 1:35–38—Jesus got up before dawn and prayed in a solitary place. Even the disciples did not know where He was. Afterward He said, "Let's go," and went about preaching in other cities. *We can fellowship with Him in solitary prayer and in preaching the Gospel.*

Luke 5:16—Jesus often withdrew from ministry to pray in the wilderness. *We can fellowship with Him by withdrawing from overtaxation of our spiritual resources.*

Luke 6:12–13—Jesus prayed all night before choosing the apostles. He obviously sought the Father's will in this historic decision. *We can fellowship with Him in prayer and in making disciples.*

Matthew 11:25–30—Jesus thanked the Father for fully knowing Him and being known of Him. Afterward He invited the "heavy laden" to come and find rest. *We can fellowship with Him in rest and in bringing others to rest.*

Matthew 15:32–39—Jesus gave thanks to the Father prior to the multiplication of the fish and loaves. Thanksgiving seems to be a factor in the release of power. *We can fellowship with Him in gratitude.*

Matthew 14:23–26—Jesus prayed all night before walking on water to come near the disciples in the storm. They thought He was a ghost (a spirit). *We can fellowship with Him in the storm.*

Luke 9:18–20—After praying alone, Jesus was joined by the disciples in prayer, and He asked them, "Who do the crowds say that I am?" Peter's revelation of Jesus as the Christ, Son of the living God, came in a prayer meeting. *We can fellowship with Him in revelation.*

John 11:38–44—Jesus gave thanks that the Father had already heard Him prior to raising Lazarus from the dead. He had obviously already prayed and knew the Father's will. *We can fellowship with Him in knowing His will and the supernatural.*

Luke 11:1–4—The disciples asked Jesus to teach them to pray. They were clearly impressed with His prayer life. He then gave them a model that differed from the prayers of the Pharisees (see Matthew 6:5–15). *We can fellowship with Him in the prayer for His Kingdom to come.*

Matthew 19:13–15—Even though the disciples tried to keep them away, Jesus prayed for children and laid His hands on them; He also commanded childlikeness. *We can fellowship with Him in blessing our children.*

Luke 22:32—Jesus prayed for Peter to have unfailing faith, and, after Peter's change of heart, that he would strengthen his brothers (see Hebrews 7:25). *We can fellowship with Him in strengthening our brothers and sisters.*

Luke 22:14–20—Jesus gave thanks before instituting the solemn New Covenant with His disciples (and with us). He blessed both bread and cup, the body and blood of Christ (see also 1 Corinthians 11:23–25). *We can fellowship with Him in the covenant life of His body and blood.*

John 17—Jesus prayed for unity in His Body, even as He and the Father are one. And He prayed that the Father would be glorified in His suffering. *We can fellowship with Him in unity with other believers and in love.*

Matthew 26:36–41—Jesus prayed prior to His trial and crucifixion. So fervent was His prayer that He even sweat drops of blood (see Luke 22:44). The disciples slept through this poignant moment. *We can fellowship in His suffering, and remain awake.*

Luke 23:34—Jesus prayed for those who crucified Him, thus fulfilling His own teaching that we should love and pray for our enemies. *We can fellowship with Him by forgiving those who misuse us and even in our being alone.*

Luke 24:49–51—Jesus was praying and blessing His disciples even as He ascended to heaven. Uppermost in Jesus' mind were the Father's will, His glory and His disciples' welfare. He instructed them to stay in Jerusalem and pray to receive the "Promise of the Father" (see Acts 1:4–8). *We can fellowship with Him in the promise of the Father.*

It is no wonder Jesus could say that all He did was what He saw the Father do. It is also no wonder that He always pleased the Father. He stayed in constant touch! (See John 5:17–30; 8:28–29.) This was also how the apostles survived awful persecutions while manifesting such power: They prayed. We cannot always be at prayer meetings, but He promised to always be with us (see Matthew 28:20). Some have said that Jesus did not teach His disciples to preach, but He did teach them to pray.

Miracles

After my study I saw miracles for seven years. We did not have one funeral even though the church grew to nearly five hundred people—and that was a miracle, too. Soon hippies came, a new experience for our suburban church. After that came people from other races, and then people from other denominations—Catholics, Episcopalians, Methodists, Pentecostals and others. Even people from groups of very questionable theology, like Theosophists, Christian Scientists and Scientologists, came to see what was happening. My ministry broadened, to say the least! During that season I was invited to speak at one of the largest Unity churches in America. Though I disagreed with them theologically, I was able to minister to them.

Then I had the opportunity to minister at a Jesuit college. This was in 1966, one year before the beginning of the Catholic charismatic renewal. I spoke to a group of students, but I had rented facilities large enough for outside youth to come. These failed to show up, and those who did come had little to give financially. Not much seemed to happen, except I lost a lot of money and learned how to plan better. "Maybe a seed was sown," I thought, but I had to cash in my insurance to pay the bills. Had I missed the Lord? I wondered.

It was years before I got the answer to that question. Our young son grew up and got a huge scholarship to that same Jesuit college, worth forty to fifty times what I lost. But that was not all. Later my granddaughter got an even larger scholarship to that same school! Thank You, Jesus! Answers do not always come immediately, nor do the rewards, but they do come. A grain of wheat can bear much fruit, if we allow it to die (see John 12:24–26).

I learned many valuable lessons from studying the prayer life of Jesus:

- We need to realize that we are talking to the Father, who loves us.
- We need to get alone to pray or pray with those who are in harmony with us.
- The secret prayer life should go beyond the public prayer life.
- There are times when prolonged prayer is necessary.
- Thanksgiving is a key to releasing the power of God.
- It is vital to pray before important decisions and events.
- Prayer is most often the situation in which God reveals Himself.
- It is in prayer that we discover God's will.
- God values childlike humility and confession of sin.

- In prayer our strength is renewed as we behold Him.

- Secret prayer can bring very public rewards.

- We cannot vindicate ourselves or escape the cross, but God is a vindicator.

The issue before us is not simply to pray more, it is to pray more effectively, and Jesus can teach us how. A key to effective prayer is forgiveness: God's forgiveness to us and our forgiveness of others. In the next chapter we will study the vital importance of forgiveness so that our prayers will not be hindered.

Discussion Questions

1. What has impressed you most about Jesus' prayer life? How can you apply it to your life?

2. What does it mean to be childlike in our prayers?

3. Why do you think thanksgiving in our prayers releases the power of God?

4. Why do you believe that Jesus is interceding for you? What does He want for you?

5. How does your private prayer life affect your public prayers?

6. Do you pray with a small group of believers? Does the presence of other people affect your candor in prayer? Should it?

7. What do you most often pray about? Can you think of ways that you might broaden your prayers?

8. What do you believe would happen if more believers prayed effectively?

5

Why Is Forgiveness So Important?

While I have been writing this book, the Lord has reminded me that only honest prayer can be effective. And sometimes it is very difficult to be honest with ourselves. Only God can show us the truth; when He does, we must respond. Pretension got the Jewish leaders in bad trouble in Jesus' day, and it led to their destruction. It still works that way today, not only because the Lord despises pretense, but because pretense causes us to ignore or be blind to things that are destroying us. We cannot pretend all is well when we hold on to unforgiveness.

I want to avoid the impression that I am "not like other men are." I am not naturally "spiritual" (naturally spiritual is an oxymoron). It takes the work of God to lead me toward spirituality. He has made me a new creation, but I have often prayed like Moses, "Please do not let me see my wretchedness." But sometimes He has. I know that I am born of His Spirit, sanctified by the Holy Spirit, a justified son of God (see 1 Thessalonians

5:23). True—I am all of that, but with flesh on. This has driven me to prayer and to wrestle with forgiveness—difficult forgiveness, which does not come easily to me.

What Is Forgiveness?

What does it mean to forgive? Jesus said to do it from your heart; I suppose that means a total release. It should mean to us whatever it means to God. We ought to find out what it means since we often ask for it.

The link between forgiveness and effective praying should be apparent to every follower of Jesus, who prayed from the cross, "Father, forgive them, for they do not know what they do" (Luke 23:34). It was obviously important to Jesus and should be to all of us who have received His forgiveness. To know that He has forgiven us is to know that we have been released from condemnation and eternal death. What greater blessing could there be? When we forgive others, it releases both them and us.

Jesus' teaching on forgiveness went beyond the Law, which said, "An eye for an eye." Jesus said, "Forgive." This contrast was very clear when Peter asked Jesus, "How often shall my brother sin against me, and I forgive him? Up to seven times?" Jesus responded with a parable: A servant was forgiven of a very large sum, but he then found someone who owed him a much smaller sum and demanded payment. When the master who had forgiven the servant heard about it, he was very angry. Turning the servant over to "the torturers," the master required that the original debt be paid. Jesus added that our Father in heaven will do the same unless we forgive our brother's trespasses from the heart (Matthew 18:21–35).

The most well-known prayer is the Lord's Prayer, our model. When the disciples requested that Jesus teach them to pray, He included, "forgive us our trespasses as we forgive those who trespass against us" in the prayer. Further along, He said, "Deliver us from the evil one." Is there a link between our forgiving others and deliverance from the evil one? I believe so; go back to Matthew 18:34, in which the unforgiving servant was delivered to the torturers.

How many people are living in some degree of spiritual stress, sickness and even torment because they refuse to forgive someone of a trespass? How many unanswered prayers might result from the failure to forgive? How many wars, small and large, are due to unforgiveness? How many have died in conflicts? We must take this issue of forgiveness more seriously so that our prayers are not hindered and so that peace is restored.

In any case we ought to forgive for our own well-being. Bitterness is like a cancer: It eats away at the one who carries it and contagiously defiles many others. Consider Esau, who was unable to repent because of his bitterness, in contrast to Jesus, who endured the cross in complete forgiveness (see Hebrews 12:3–17).

Once I was hurting over what I felt was unjust treatment by fellow Christians. I prayed, "Lord, I hurt." I believe the Holy Spirit spoke to me immediately: *What hurts isn't dead yet.* In that moment I understood that my pain would cease if I died to myself.

The beauty is that the Lord has given to us the power to forgive, not just the command (see John 20:23). We can do it. And what forgiveness can accomplish is amazing. We can be released when we release; we can be forgiven when we forgive; we can access the Father and be delivered from the evil one. We can be healed. As we show mercy, we find mercy, and our offerings become acceptable. Unity and reconciliation are accomplished, and the power of God is released. With forgiveness comes a host of blessings and joys.

Experiencing Forgiveness

I remember when I first experienced forgiveness, at my salvation experience. I was young but well aware of my sinful nature. Our church had a series of revival services, and the Holy Spirit was convicting people of their sins, which is what happens when He moves (see John 16:7–11). The evangelist was preaching about hell like he had just gotten back from there himself.

"If you need to accept Jesus as your Lord and Savior, raise your hand." Without a thought my hand went up. After the service, he led me to a side room, and there he opened the Scriptures regarding sin, repentance, forgiveness and salvation. He read John 3:16–18, Romans 3:23 and Romans 6:23. He explained that salvation was a gift from God, one I did not deserve. He read 1 John 1:7–10 and explained that if I confessed my sin, accepted Jesus' death in my place and trusted in Him, then I would be forgiven, cleansed and born again. We prayed and I accepted Jesus, believing that He had taken my sin on the cross and removed it from me. I was free, forgiven and cleansed.

It was all that the evangelist said it would be, but at the time, I did not realize that the forgiveness I had received would be the forgiveness I would have to give. Time, the Holy Spirit and God's Word would teach me that profound reality. I could not always *make* peace, but I could *have* peace if I forgave.

So, before we pray or partake in Lord's supper, we must examine ourselves and forgive lest we bring condemnation on ourselves. God is a holy and forgiving God; His body and His blood are not to be received into an unforgiving heart and body (see 1 Corinthians 11:17–34). As you have received grace, give it. Pray for your enemies, those who have misused you, and so fulfill the law of Christ (see Romans 13:8–10; 1 Corinthians 13).

Bringing It Home

Unfortunately, we do not always fulfill the law of Christ—at least, I have not. Husbands are to *always* love their wives as Christ loved the Church and gave Himself for it (see Ephesians 5:25–32). I regret to say that I believed it and preached it, but I often failed to give that grace as Christ did. Here is a rather embarrassing example.

I like breakfast—eggs, coffee, toast—then I am out the door to work on the important things in a pastor's life. My wife, on the other hand, loved peace and approached the kitchen casually. She never cared for eggs or coffee, and the Lord, in His humor, put us together. So it was one morning that she found the kitchen but forgot to put coffee grounds in the coffee maker and slightly burned the toast. I sat down to hot water and burnt toast. The toast was not the only thing burnt.

Being the "Spirit-filled" man that I was, I gave her the Word of the Lord—Lord Charles, that is—and left for the office. I left her feeling like a failure and, I am sure, in tears. Between the house and office, something mysterious and awesome happens to a man of my vocation: You become a "clergyman"—think Clark Kent turning into Superman. Your whole countenance and disposition change. You become wise, patient and pleasant, and so it was when I arrived at the office.

My usual procedure was to begin the day with staff prayer. As I knelt, I felt that I heard a voice say, *What are you doing?* "I'm about to pray," I responded. *To whom?* the voice asked. "To You; I'm going to pray to You, Lord." *Not today: The shop is closed. You have work to do at home.* And I knew that it was the Lord. I excused myself and went home to a surprised wife. Then I apologized for my sorry behavior and asked her forgiveness. She needed to hear that, but I needed to say it even more. The reward was not only her forgiveness but the Lord's. I do not know what would have happened had I not obeyed. What did happen was that it had a positive effect on both our lives, and grace was given to me.

Forgiveness on a Grand Scale

While I often need forgiveness, I have not always been quick to give it. Case in point: For one of the greatest seasons in my life, I worked in a close fellowship with other Bible teachers. As a team we traveled, spoke at great conferences, published a great magazine with over one hundred thousand readers and owned a television station. We even made a pilgrimage to Belgium, where we traveled with a cardinal and other leaders to Rome, had an audience with the Pope, at which he introduced us as his "ecumenical brethren," and then went to Israel to see many holy sites. It was a month-long tour of holy places with holy people.

But things happen on the way to heaven. Controversy had surrounded our group from the very beginning of our association in 1970; it arose from our partnership and the things that we taught, like baptism in the Holy Spirit, worship, deliverance from evil spirits (and how it was done), covenant relationships, biblical family, discipleship, submission to authority and honoring servants of God. We were no experts; we were just trying to practice what we saw in the New Testament. We were not, however, at all prepared for the consequences.

One consequence is that when you teach or preach with anointing, people come to you for a spiritual reward. We grew a following, though that was not our purpose—we had just come together for mutual accountability. It turns out that others wanted mutual accountability, too, and they sought us for help. In 1975 we helped lead a meeting of five thousand leaders, and in 1977 we helped convene a meeting in Arrowhead Stadium in Kansas City with nearly fifty thousand people. But that was only the beginning. From 1970 until 1985, approximately one hundred thousand people came from the United States and abroad to associate with us, wanting to be shepherded and discipled. Were we ready for that responsibility? Of course not. While our messages were true (and still are), and we did the best we knew how, we made lots of errors. Besides that, most of us were teachers, not pastors. I was and still am a pastor by calling, but never on that scale.

Another consequence was fierce opposition against us teachers, which led to controversies that disrupted churches and friendships, even spreading across America and to other nations. Some Christian leaders used television, radio, magazines, books and audio tapes to denounce us and the people who followed us, often labeling us a cult (at this time the Jim Jones tragedy was still fresh in people's thinking). Numerous reconciliation meetings followed that mostly failed. In 1985 I and the other teachers agreed to dissolve our mutual commitment in order to bring peace to our families and to the larger Church.[1] We were on our own again.

I accepted the necessity of "uncoupling" our commitments, but I carried a lot of anger inside, which took a toll on me. As leader of the covering organization that shouldered the responsibility, I was left with a $750,000 building mortgage and a magazine that was losing $350,000 each year. Some of the other teachers issued public apologies for our mistakes, as did I. I felt it very important not to deny the truth that we had taught or betray those who had sacrificed to join us, but for some, that was not enough. One day Carolyn finally said, "I'm tired of hearing you apologize." I agreed, but I was unaware that I had unresolved anger and perhaps unforgiveness deep inside.

1. Several years back, Dr. S. David Moore wrote a book about our association, called *The Shepherding Movement*, that I believe accurately portrays its history.

Facing the Truth

Years went by, and one December I was ministering in a church in California. I had come prepared, or so I thought. The spiritual intensity of the worship service got very high, and the Lord spoke to me: *You don't have the right message.* That is a startling thing to hear when you are about to preach. I tried to rebuke the thought, but it would not go away. Finally I said, "If this is You, Lord, what will I preach?" Instantly, the Lord gave me a fresh message, a clear outline and confidence. I had peace.

Then the Lord spoke again: *But I will not bless you unless you agree now to write three letters and ask forgiveness.* Then He gave me the names of three people: two had formerly been my fellow teachers, and the third was a journalist and friend who had offended me in a book, in articles and even in a letter to my wife. I swallowed hard, but who wants to get up and preach without God's help? I had done that before—not fun. So I promised the Lord that I would ask forgiveness of my friends.

As soon as I got home, I wrote letters to those three people, asking forgiveness for my anger. I had forgiven, but I also needed forgiveness. All three responded. The journalist forgave me and asked for forgiveness himself for writing with a "poisoned pen"; two weeks later, he died. I did not even know that he was sick.

The Rewards

There are many rewards to forgiveness: the ability to pray and be heard, the release of our burdens and others' burdens, healing, deliverance from oppression and depression, reconciliation, harmony, peace, the fresh release of the Gospel as at Pentecost, fellowship with Jesus the Forgiver, a new focus on the real issues of life, enemies who become friends, a better family, children who grow up happy, a prosperous life with God's peace and less conflict and turmoil (see Psalm 133). How much is all that worth? The price is not really that high given the rewards. It is simply a matter of humbling ourselves and saying things from the heart like, "I'm sorry," "I forgive and ask your forgiveness," and, importantly, "Let's go have communion together."

Forgiveness is vital to effective prayer, and in future chapters we will explore further heart attitudes that enable us to please our Father in prayer—for instance, what elements in our prayers move God?

Discussion Questions

1. What does forgiveness mean to you?

2. Why should you forgive?

3. Why do we fail to forgive?

4. What are some benefits of forgiveness?

5. What are some results of unforgiveness? Bitterness?

6. What if the Lord does not forgive us?

7. In what way is the Lord's forgiveness of Peter's denial a model to us?

8. Do you know anyone whom you should forgive? How about starting with all who are in authority? That is who we are told to pray for first. How about family members, neighbors, fellow Christians, even pastors?

6

How Does God Want Me to Pray?

Is it really all that important to think about how God wants us to pray? Of course it is. He is God, the sovereign who will hear us and hopefully grant our petition. Whether or not our prayer is effective depends on what He decides. Pleasing Him in prayer is paramount, not pleasing ourselves.

As I previously stated, my earliest memories are of swamps and bayous. I was born into a far different culture than the ones I was introduced to in the following years. Each introduction has required adjustments—sometimes embarrassing and difficult ones.

I was six years old when we moved to rural south Alabama, a very different place. It was a little more open, and the people were mostly Baptist instead of Catholic. They were still rural, agrarian and hardworking. I learned to dig potatoes, cut cabbage, pull corn, cut meat, drive a truck at the age of fourteen and do other things that farm boys do. Then, at age twenty, I became a pastor in a nice suburb of the city. The people were "new money" and moving upward. They were still hardworking, but social class was much more important.

After seven years, I became involved in spiritual, personal and Church renewal; that took me to a whole new world. Sometimes my thinking was still in the swamps, though my appearance had changed. Now I was speaking to Catholics, Methodists, Episcopalians, Presbyterians, Pentecostals, businessmen's organizations and other diverse groups. On occasion I also spoke to "old money" people, a situation as far from the home of my childhood as one could get. Added to the wealthy were people with power (including the cardinal who lived in the bishop's palace in Brussels). I was still the country boy with the south Alabama accent. I did not have a clue about the way they thought, but I would learn—sometimes the hard way. We learn little if we remain only among those who think just as we do.

Looking Up with Gratitude

Let me give you an example of how those adjustments affected my prayer life. In 1965 I was invited to another city to speak at a meeting in someone's home. It was a large home owned by a banker and his wife. They were definitely "old money" and probably owned much of the bank. The evening before my engagement, we sat down to a formal candlelit dinner with more utensils than I had ever seen; I certainly did not know which to use or when to use them. The other guest was the dean of Anglican priests in western Canada. He was perfectly comfortable. The maid knew far more than I did (and probably understood my plight). I watched what everyone else did and tried to follow suit.

At the end of the several-course meal, my host announced he and his wife would be leaving early the next morning. He invited me to sleep in and said the maid would prepare breakfast and take care of any needs I might have. So it was that I came downstairs after they had left to find the maid ready to serve me. That in and of itself was a new experience. She did her task with excellence, quietly preparing and serving a beautiful breakfast (also with several courses). I enjoy breakfast, and that one was a work of art. I was happy to be alone to enjoy it without the anxiety of maintaining proprieties.

Breakfast concluded, I wanted to express my thanks, but in doing so I made a horrible mistake: I called her by the evening maid's name, not even realizing that it was a different woman. Having been a part of the family for many years, she understood my problem; she was confident of her place, but I was not confident of mine. She put her hands on her hips and looked at me. "Boy, you are just like a hog under an acorn tree. You're just eating the acorns and never looking up to see where they come from!"

I was chastened and embarrassed, and she was right. The Lord spoke to me: *Write that on your heart!* Gratitude is realizing where your blessings come from. Ingratitude can quench the source.

King David entered God's gates with thanksgiving in his heart (see Psalm 100:4). Thanksgiving is much more than mere words or moving to the beat of a catchy tune. It is instead a deep awareness of who He is, who we are and the fact that He would be in our lives. I am grateful that the God of all things would condescend to men of low estate—to a swamp person in the palace of the divine King! To a person born in sin and made righteous by holy blood, an heir of Christ and joint heir *with* Christ (see Romans 8:17)—what riches!

Gratitude comes out of the deep awareness of God's grace and mercy. It flows like a river from springs of humility and releases the great potential in the human heart. It also releases the unlimited favor of our wealthy Father who owns all the silver and gold, the cattle on a thousand hills. Gratitude keeps grace flowing.

My daughter, Charlyn, has worked with children in Costa Rica since the early 1990s. She and Enrique have adopted five children, siblings who had three different fathers and a mother who willingly gave them up. They had lived in a shack of tin and wood, with dirt floors, a leaky roof and no indoor plumbing. Now they live in a beautiful, loving home with parents and two sisters (Charlyn and Enrique's girls), made possible by God's grace and faithful friends of the mission. I enjoy visiting them as often as possible. What I deeply appreciate is how they say, "Thank you, Grandpa!" because I know it comes from the heart. They look up at the "acorn tree."

Sometimes I take them to a very nice restaurant just to see how much they appreciate it. We are a very diverse group: two African-Jamaican sons, one son of Hispanic descent, two Latina daughters and two mixed daughters. When I walk into a restaurant with my Anglo daughter, Hispanic son-in-law and seven multiethnic grandchildren, we catch stares. But I am full of joy to see their joy and gratitude. Is God like that as He sees us dining on His largesse? I hope so. Gratitude comes from the heart, the deepest recesses of our own being. We enjoy the blessings, but even more we love the Tree of Life.

Praise Is the Fruit

Psalm 100:4 continues, "Enter . . . into His courts with praise." Praise is not only a step *further* into His presence, it is a step *up* into His presence. True gratitude is the awareness of who He is and His mercy toward us; praise is the fruit of our lips, the natural overflow of the heart when we realize who He truly is. Thanksgiving is the seed; praise is the fruit (see Hebrews 13:15).

David, a humble shepherd boy who became the powerful king of Israel, excelled in both thanksgiving and praise. When you look up the word *praise* in a concordance, you discover that David used it more than anyone else in Scripture. A friend once said, "Mercy is when we do *not* get what we do deserve; grace is when we *do* get what we do not deserve." David's praise sprang out of the realization of God's loving-kindness (see Psalm 63:3–5).

One of the tragedies of life is realizing too late the One who helped us on our journey and made success possible. If we do not turn our hearts to praise the Lord for all He has done, we will be more impressed by the things of this world than the things of God.

My early years were spent among people who worked hard simply to survive. They did their duty and expected you to do the same, and praise was rare. Our culture had not learned much about affirmation and self-esteem, and children were not considered little "gods" to be adored; they were future field hands to be trained. My parents loved me, but as far as I know, they were not overly impressed with me.

Since becoming an adult I am not easily impressed, except by God and the works of His hands. Of course, I am *sometimes* impressed with certain individuals and their performance, and praise is certainly good when warranted; but the "everybody gets a trophy" mentality is *not* reality. This is how praise becomes mere flattery and is cheapened. Praise can become so cheap that the only one who takes it seriously is the one receiving it—and sometimes not even the recipient is buying it.

Our culture is too impressed with petty things and not nearly impressed enough with God, who has surpassed all in who He is and what He has done. Now, God *can* make your jaw drop open. He did it to me when He healed my friend's wife, who had been in a wheelchair 22 years with a severed spinal column following an accident. She now walks! Some words need to be reserved for God; *awesome* is one such word. Being overly impressed with human nature—especially with ourselves—is a formula for disappointment. Being impressed with God is a formula for worship.

Worship

Here again, in worship, David excelled: "Oh come, let us worship and bow down; let us kneel before the LORD our Maker" (under His care) (Psalm 95:6). Worship is the recognition that God is the Supreme One and we are the dependent ones who bow and prostrate ourselves before His majesty. Gratitude and praise bring us into worship, the third dimension of complete surrender. Our lives are now His.

Worship is more than a church service, singing, giving and all the other accoutrements of religion; it is a life laid down before the Creator and Redeemer of our lives. It is saying with the apostle, "I have been crucified with Christ; it is no longer I who live, but Christ lives in me; and the life which I now live in the flesh I live by faith in the Son of God, who loved me and gave Himself for me" (Galatians 2:20).

The reason that I can have access to the most holy place is because the Father tore the veil in the Temple, and in heaven, when Jesus died on the cross (see Matthew 27:51). We can all have access into His presence, where every creature at hand is bowing down before Him, by the redeeming and justifying blood of Christ. Casual? Don't even think about it.

The first time I quit seminary, I had been taking a course on the gospels and realized that we had spent no time talking about the *reason* for the cross. This upset me, as I believed that the cross was the central point of history and the basis of my salvation. After the last session of the course, I went to the professor and asked him about the cross and its meaning. "Don't you believe that Jesus died in our place? Don't you believe in substitutionary atonement?"

He said that he did not and gave what was to me an incoherent explanation. I was stunned. I left for our one-room efficiency apartment in disbelief. I was driving a thousand miles a week, commuting from the church that I pastored to prepare for a better ministry. It was a sacrifice, and my professor did not even believe in the basis for my sacrifice.

When I arrived at my apartment in anger and dismay, I tossed my Bible on the couch and knelt before it, sobbing and praying. "Lord, if he is right, I have no message; if he is wrong, I have no business here." I will never forget pouring out my dilemma and disappointment. Finally, from my knees I looked up to see my Bible open before me, as though it had been placed there. I began to read.

> But Christ came as High Priest of the good things to come, with the greater and more perfect tabernacle not made with hands, that is, not of this creation. Not with the blood of goats and calves, but with His own blood He entered the Most Holy Place once for all, having obtained eternal redemption.
>
> Hebrews 9:11–12

The chapter goes on to explain that His death brought me life and established the New Covenant with me. His blood paid the price for my sin and made a bond with God. I felt like shouting.

That was a seminal moment for me. Years later I was privileged and honored by Jack Hayford to write the commentary notes on those very verses in the *Spirit-Filled Life Bible*.

What an amazing reality: We can, through thanksgiving, praise and worship, enter the most holy place—the heavenly Temple—by the blood of Jesus Christ. There is power in the blood of the Lamb. That is high worship. We can join the angels, the Church triumphant and all of heaven in the presence of our Creator.

United in Worship

One Sunday morning after my wife departed to be with the Lord, I was still feeling her loss deeply, even in the middle of our church's worship service. Then the presence of God entered the building in a way that I knew He was there. In that moment I understood something that brought great comfort: She was there too. We were both in His presence worshiping. I was in the Church militant, while she was in the Church triumphant—both of us one in worship. True worship is the essence of unity both here and in eternity.

We can please God in prayer by maintaining an attitude of thanksgiving, praise and worship. Now that we have addressed these and other foundational aspects of prayer (such as what prayer is, who God is and the essentialness of forgiveness), we will turn to the vital role of faith in God as we pray.

—————— Discussion Questions ——————

1. What is the danger of using a formula for prayer?

2. What elements seem most important to you in your prayer life?

3. How is the Temple a model for prayer?

4. Can you name occasions when you knew that God was hearing your prayer?

5. Why is it important to know that God is hearing your prayer?

6. Why is gratitude so significant? Praise? Worship?

7. How do you worship in your prayers?

8. Why is unity important to prayer (see Psalm 133)?

7

How Important Is Faith When I Pray?

Two of my favorite books are *The Real Faith* by Charles Price and *Smith Wigglesworth: The Complete Collection of His Life Teachings*. Both books are about pioneers in healing and miracles, and they both point out that faith is a gift from God. Price calls faith a "grace," saying, "We have taken faith out of the realm of the spiritual and, without realizing just what we are doing, have put it in the realm of the metaphysical."[1] Price goes on to explore the difference between mental assent and spiritual gift.

Wigglesworth was referred to as the "apostle of faith." He is said to have raised numerous people from the dead and observed the healing of thousands. I have tremendous respect for both men and recommend a study of their experiences. If we want to understand what faith is, we can also turn to Hebrews 11, perhaps the greatest chapter in the Bible about faith. In it the

1. Charles Price, *The Real Faith* (Pasadena: Charles S. Price Publishing, 1940), 5.

writer not only defines faith but offers numerous examples of people who exercised it.

According to Hebrews 11:1, "Faith is the substance of things hoped for, the evidence of things not seen." It is a substantive confidence, a realization of something that has not yet occurred (see verse 3). Without faith, we cannot please God: "For he who comes to God must believe that He is, and that He is a rewarder of those who diligently seek Him" (verse 6).

What kind of faith gets us to those rewards? Note that faith is a deep and clear conviction from God; we are asking Him to give, knowing that He desires to give. James tells us that faith is not double minded (see James 1:6–8); rather it is confidence in the outcome, which can only be brought about by a single-minded conviction regarding the will of God (see 1 John 4:14–15). Faith demands trust. A friend once told me, "Faith is what God gives us; trust is what we give Him." I believe that this confidence comes by being in His presence and knowing the will of God; it is not borne of the human spirit but by the Holy Spirit. If we need help, we can look to Jesus, the author and finisher of our faith (see Hebrews 12:2).

Natural Faith

There are many kinds of faith, beginning with "natural faith," the belief in something better. This lives in the hearts of most people. It has a real effect in our lives and the lives of those around us; it could be called "positive thinking," and it has power and brings rewards. But that is not the same as faith in God or the faith of God.

I believed that I could play football and even that I could be a quarterback, though I was small and relatively slow. But I could not. Then I believed I could be a running back. I could not do that either, but I still believed I could play somewhere. Finally, I became a guard—a "fullback with his brains kicked out." I was a good guard and made All-County. But that was just my natural faith and determination (though God did teach me through it). It is easy to get natural faith and real faith confused, and many do, but the differences become apparent in the results.

Biblical Faith

The book of Romans is another great book on faith; Romans 10:17 tells us that "faith comes by hearing, and hearing by the word of God." Some translations say, "Hearing a word from God." Scripture reveals the overall will of God, but God also speaks to us through His Word; we need to "hear God" in it. When we hear God in His Word as we study it, our hearing becomes the foundation for our faith.

The authority and authenticity of Scripture have been relentlessly attacked by some, but to let ourselves be diminished in our confidence in the Bible or dull in our hearing is to be diminished in our faith. Never listen to those who infect with the terrible virus of doubt; they will destroy your foundation for faith. Entire denominations have been wrecked by degrading the holy Word, and with them millions of lives.

Faith is a gift from God (see 1 Corinthians 12:9). It grows as we study the Word, listen to the Holy Spirit and listen to the testimonies of those who have demonstrated real faith—a substantive confidence in something not yet made visible.

Following the Cloud

When God moves upon and speaks to us, He challenges us to take a new step into the unknown. Our salvation and justification come by faith in Jesus Christ, but we also live by faith in what He tells us. Every step into the proceeding will of God is a step of faith that pleases Him. Habakkuk 2:4 says, "The just shall live by his faith" (see also Romans 1:17; Hebrews 10:38). Faith is the motivator that powers our journey into the will of God.

In 1971 I became convinced that the Lord wanted Carolyn and me to move to Fort Lauderdale, Florida, with our two young children. My entire life had been lived in Louisiana and Alabama, and in Mississippi for college—these were southern cultures. I had pastored in Mobile, Alabama, for fourteen years—seven years before personal renewal and seven years after. The church had grown and we were comfortable. We had filled the civic theater with guests, well-known evangelists like David Wilkerson and Nicky Cruz. Many people came to Christ and were filled with the Holy Spirit. But the Lord was "taking the feathers out of my nest"; I had to fly.

One late night my wife came to me in fear. "Someone was trying to get into the window." My car was in the shop at the time, and to a passerby, it would have appeared that she was home alone with our young children. I could not believe that someone was breaking in, since the Lord always protected us. I leaned heavily on Psalm 91, especially as I traveled often. But I went to the window. As I drew back the drapes, I came face-to-face with the intruder, who was just on the other side of the windowpane.

I shouted, "In the name of Jesus!" He was a large man, but he was frightened by my appearing at the window. He ran over the chain-link fence in our backyard, bending it to the ground. I returned to my room, shaken, and got my Bible. The intruder had not entered our house, but fear had. I opened my Bible to Psalm 91. "He who dwells in the secret place of the Most High shall abide under the shadow of the Almighty. I will say of the LORD, 'He is my refuge and my fortress; my God, in Him I will trust'" (verses 1–2). Verse 5 adds, "You shall not be afraid of the terror by night."

Then I heard the Lord say, *The cloud is moving.* I immediately thought of the clouds that covered Israel, leading them through the wilderness and sheltering them from the terrible heat. That cloud had covered me and my family, and now it was moving. I had to move with His presence.

Mountains Moved by Faith

I had not wanted to move. I liked the home we were renting; it was near Carolyn's family and mine. My office was within walking distance. Everything that we needed was there, except the will of God. I flew to Fort Lauderdale to consult with fellow Bible teachers who also lived there, and they confirmed that the Lord wanted us to come. I boarded a plane to fly home.

The plane waited a long while on the tarmac, and I passed time by reading Alvin Toffler's new book, *Future Shock.*[2] As I read, my eyes fell on this line: "Meanwhile, one haunting question remains, is Fort Lauderdale the future?" I shut the book, not believing what I had just read, but there it was! When I opened the book again, it was still there.

In a few days Carolyn and I drove to Fort Lauderdale, leaving our two young children with grandparents. Upon arriving we contacted a recommended real estate agent, who, after hearing what we could afford, showed us every chicken coop in Fort Lauderdale. We were dispirited.

At almost ten o'clock that night we knelt in our motel room to seek the Lord. Had we missed Him somehow? Should we go home and take our chances? I prayed, "But, Lord, we believe that You told us to come here."

We prayed and waited. Soon I felt that the Lord was telling me to get in the car and drive south; we got on I-95 and drove

2. Alvin Toffler, *Future Shock* (New York: Bantam Books, 1971), 123.

into Hollywood, just south of Fort Lauderdale. We felt peace. Passing by several homes with for-sale signs, Carolyn said, "I feel like we could live here." "Me too," I agreed. Faith began to grow as we obeyed.

We saw evening phone numbers on some of the for-sale signs, so we pulled up to a 7-Eleven, where I used the pay phone to call one of the numbers. It was 10:30 p.m., and I woke the agent up. "I'm just around the corner from you," he said. "I'll be there shortly." And he was. "My brother is a Bible teacher. I'll do all I can to help you." And he did.

He showed us a vacant new house with three bedrooms, two bathrooms and a swimming pool. "This is not the one you'll buy; the one I'll show you tomorrow is just like it, pool and all, but people live there so I'll show it to you in the morning." He was amazingly confident.

The house he showed us the next morning was indeed as nice as the previous one, plus it was landscaped and had drapes and other amenities that we could not have afforded. We thanked the owner and left with the real estate agent. As we rounded the corner, he parked the car. "What is the absolute largest check you can write for a down payment?" he asked. I hesitated. "Four thousand dollars."

He paused a moment. "This is going to be tight, but write the check and give it to me. I'm going to tell the owner who you are and what you do; then I'll hand him the check. He'll get angry, but he won't be able to turn the check loose. You take a walk, and I'll pick you up and let you know as soon as he gives me the answer." I handed him the check and he left, while we took a walk in a strange land, wondering. The agent returned in about thirty minutes. "Well, it is just like I said." We would be homeowners in Hollywood, and Fort Lauderdale was our future.

I can assure you that ours was not "natural faith"; it was simply obedience to what we had heard from the Lord. In the months to come, we would more than double the return on our investment. What faith we had came by hearing God and obeying. Through the years that have followed, I have heard and experienced many stories of faith. Ministries like mine and yours have emerged from simple steps into the unknown, like Abraham's journey.

The Power of Faith

Next to the love of God, faith is the most powerful force. Faith pleases God because He is faithful and true. Pleasing God gives us access to His power. By faith our forefathers accomplished through Him all that we have inherited. Faith gives us the power to see into God's presence and purpose; then it gives us vision, so that we can see into what does not yet exist and see it come to pass. It delivers us from the evil one, heals the sick and, yes, even raises the dead. Faith precedes and performs miracles and secures provision. It leads us into the harvest and secures lives for the Kingdom of God; it turns on lights in the darkness, and it is contagious. My prayer is that your testimony of God's work in your life will cause others to embark on a life of faith.

One day, a phone call came to our church office. It was a request to visit a woman who was dying of cancer. She had gotten down to 85 pounds, and the family was not Christian. I was out of town, so my associate, John Duke, went to the hospital to anoint her with oil and pray for her. The scene was sad when he arrived. The father had lifted her up and taken her to the window to wave to her young children below. After he placed her back in the bed, John anointed her with oil and prayed for her in a God-given faith; then he left. A little while later we got word that she had been healed and the family had accepted Jesus Christ. That experience was overflowing with rewards:

a mother returned to her little children, a wife returned to her husband and a family returned to Christ.

In the same season I was asked to go to the hospital to pray for a woman who was having a mental breakdown. Her condition was so severe that she was restrained to the hospital bed. As I stood by her bed, she was trying to catch things flying through the air, things that were not there. In a moment of silence, waiting and not knowing what to say, the Holy Spirit came down upon her and me; she focused her eyes on me. Faith came with the Holy Spirit. I prayed a brief prayer and left. The next day when I returned, she was sitting up clothed and in her right mind. Her nurse even came to Christ. The presence of God brings faith.

I do not disparage medical help. My father-in-law was a man of faith and a physician. We often talked about healing, and he often prayed about his patients. Faith and healing are still a mystery to me, but I can only do in faith what I see the Father do (see John 5:19, 30). When I do, good things happen.

I often pray the prayer of the father who came to Jesus on his son's behalf: "Immediately the father of the child cried out and said with tears, 'Lord, I believe; help my unbelief!'" (Mark 9:24). The Lord healed the son. This story tells me that it is okay to admit our need for more faith, and that God will answer an honest prayer. He gave faith, the father sought Jesus and Jesus' faith healed the boy. This father is also a reminder that we should all desire more and that Jesus is the source—much depends on our growing in faith. If we ask the Lord, we will receive. Bear in mind that we do not control the Lord with our faith. He guides us by the faith that He gives us, and He has given to every believer a measure of faith (see Romans 12:3; Ephesians 4:7). If we exercise our faith, He will give more.

The good news is that our faith can grow as we study God's Word and as we pray in the Holy Spirit. Jude testifies to this when he says, "But you, beloved, building yourselves up on your most holy faith, praying in the Holy Spirit" (Jude 20). In the next chapter we will discuss what it means to "pray in the Holy Spirit."

Discussion Questions

1. How would you describe faith?

2. What is the difference between natural and spiritual faith?

3. How can we grow in faith?

4. What do you see as the main purpose of faith?

5. How do you deal with doubt?

6. What is the difference between "the faith" and "our faith"? (See Jude 3.)

7. What are the rewards of faith?

8

What Does It Mean to Pray in the Holy Spirit?

Captains of seafaring ships are highly skilled and highly trained; they know the ship, and they know the sea. They also know the crew and the capabilities of each crew member, upon which precious cargo depends. Captains have not only great capability but great power—the ship is definitely not a democracy. The captain is responsible for the ship, the crew and the cargo; everyone else takes orders.

But when the ship has passed through the ocean to its destination and approaches the harbor, another pilot takes the ship's wheel, a local harbor pilot. This pilot is not only skilled but knows the local channel, the reefs, the sandbars, the tides, the currents and how to bring the ship safely to the dock. As the ship approaches the harbor, its captain must relinquish the wheel to the harbor pilot. No doubt he does so with concern, but also with trust, as he steps aside and gives control to someone more skilled in piloting boats through that harbor.

So it is in our prayer life. We have been in control, navigating our lives to this point. Self-control is very important, but at some point we will approach an area of life foreign to us. We have charts to follow and knowledge to rely on, as we should. But our natural mind, which has been our "captain" up to this point, is not native to the realm of the Spirit, the invisible realm of God. We must allow another pilot to come aboard and take over. He knows the way to the throne of God.

A person can be an expert on religion and know the Bible without knowing or understanding the realm of the Spirit. Such was the case with Nicodemus, a ruler of the Jews and a Pharisee, who came to Jesus one night to inquire because he had witnessed miracles. Though he was an "expert" on the Bible and Jewish law, he did not understand the realm of the Spirit.

Jesus told this thoroughly educated and religious man that in order to see and enter the kingdom of God, he had to be born from above. He needed not only a natural birth but also a spiritual rebirth. This puzzled Nicodemus, as it does many in our time. Jesus went on to liken the Holy Spirit to the wind. We can hear its sound and feel its force, but we cannot see it or control it.

So it is with those who are born of the Spirit; they are moved by an invisible power. He is the other pilot who takes over, who has knowledge beyond our skilled intellect, to guide us in prayer (see John 3:1–12). Jesus came in order to open that realm to us, and He sent the Holy Spirit to guide us in it. We must relinquish our command to Him. Yes, we have a choice, but we must choose His guidance in order to enter His domain—to approach His throne.

My Choice

I understand the difficulty of this choice, having been something of a Pharisee myself. I believed and studied the Bible. I debated doctrine, often in a harsh, unforgiving manner, and was overly confident in my own understanding. I did not, however, see miracles, and I often heard others say the days when God worked miracles ended long ago. But I had reached an impasse; at age 27, I knew that my own ability had reached its limits, and I became open to the possibility that more was available. I could "sail the seas," but I could not deliver the cargo that I saw in the Bible and believed in. I had been born again and sometimes felt "the wind of the Spirit," but I had not handed over the wheel of my life.

The risks on both sides were great: I could continue my own journey, risking the rocks and missing the channel, or give my life over to the Holy Spirit to guide me through the unknown. I finally chose the latter. One day, as I was praying alone in my office, I felt the wind of the Spirit powerfully, and words that I did not comprehend came pouring out of my mouth like a torrent. No, I did not lose control. Rather I gave control to the force that I felt, and it swept me into a new world of joy and peace. For about thirty minutes I could not articulate my joy and wonder.

I had studied Scriptures about the Holy Spirit, even with great interest and intensity, but this demonstrated the promise of Jesus to me. John the Baptist had said that Jesus would baptize with the Holy Spirit and fire; that is what I believed I experienced. Jesus had been filled with and led by the Holy Spirit, and He did great miracles. I think that is what every serious Christian inwardly desires. The evidence of that great release was apparent in my life, my family and my church, though I did not openly discuss it until I was asked several months later. But daily I was getting into the Word and the Spirit and praying with the Holy Spirit. I was invested, and like Nicodemus I was thirsty to know Jesus better.

The Promise

Jesus never intended His disciples to walk in His way on their own. Knowing they would need a Helper, Jesus prepared the disciples for their own encounter with the mighty wind of the Spirit (see John 14–16). Shortly before His ascension, He reminded them of the "promise of the Father" that He had previously described, commanding them to go to Jerusalem to wait for it. In Acts 1:8, He told them what the result would be: They would become witnesses to Him to the very ends of the earth. In the Holy Spirit, He would be with them always.

The disciples obeyed and returned to the same Upper Room where Jesus had inaugurated the New Covenant. They waited, sorting out their issues and selecting an apostle to take Judas' place (they settled on Matthias). Whatever else might have happened, they came into one accord, with complete harmony in their desire to obey the Lord and in their focus on the promise. They waited through desperation over the physical absence of Jesus and the nearby presence of His crucifiers. They awaited the unknown. These issues greatly motivated them. They were confident in Jesus and His word to them, if not in themselves. What was going to happen? How would they know that the promise had been received? They waited and waited and waited some more.

Finally, the feast of Pentecost arrived, a celebration of the day hundreds of years earlier when the Lord gave the Law to Moses. We do not know all that happened to Moses at that time, but we do know that he was on top of a mountain, in the cloud of God's presence, and that when he came down, his face shown so brightly that he had to put a veil over it. Centuries later, Jerusalem was packed with thousands of Jews gathered from other nations and Israel for this celebration. Meanwhile the disciples, gathered in the Upper Room, were waiting for another visitation from God.

It was early in the morning on the day of Pentecost when the promise came. Suddenly there came a sound from heaven like a mighty rushing wind, filling the whole house. Flames of fire appeared and sat on each of them. And they were all filled with the Holy Spirit and began to speak in languages they did not know, as the Spirit gave them utterance (see Acts 2:2–4).

In an instant, the timid disciples, who had fled the cross and doubted the resurrection of Jesus, became bold, fearless and loud. They were heard outside the building, and those from other nations heard them speaking in their own languages. A large crowd gathered, and some thought the disciples were intoxicated. Meanwhile, others asked, "What does this mean?"

Then Peter stood with the now-united disciples and began to preach the Good News that Jesus was the risen Lord. He warned the Jews to save themselves from their wicked and corrupt generation, prompting the people to cry, "What must we do to be saved?" Peter answered, "Repent, and let every one of you be baptized in the name of Jesus Christ for the remission of sins; and you shall receive the gift of the Holy Spirit" (Acts 2:38). Then he added, "For the promise is to you and to your children, and to all who are afar off, as many as the Lord our God will call" (verse 39).

Power to Be Witnesses

That day, three thousand people were added to the Church; these continued in one accord in the apostles' teaching, breaking bread together in joy and fellowship and praising God every day. The Lord added daily to their numbers, and great acts of God were occurring. Experiences like this continued to occur, as recorded in Acts, throughout the New Testament (see Acts 10, 19; Ephesians 5:18) and throughout history.

Some have argued that such experiences "ceased" when the last apostle died, in spite of the very words of the apostle Peter in Acts 2:39 or the words of Paul in 1 Corinthians 12 and 14, or in Ephesians 5:18. The ideology of cessation has robbed us of the "promise of the Father" and the power of the Holy Spirit.

It has stolen untold lives, souls and rewards that the Lord died and rose again for us to receive.

Accounts of the Moravians and Charles Finney were two examples from history that confirmed to me that cessation was wrong. The Holy Spirit visited the Moravians on August 13, 1727, in Herrnhut, Germany. These men and women were followers of John Hus (1373–1415), the martyred Bohemian reformer, and they faced persecution and death. They had gathered to Herrnhut at the invitation of a young Christian nobleman, Count von Zinzendorf, who offered them asylum. Zinzendorf's estate became a sanctuary where they gathered to seek the Lord, and there He powerfully visited them. Reading Zinzendorf's life story opened my eyes.

Then I read about the life of Charles G. Finney (1792–1875), the powerful evangelist during the Second Great Awakening. After his conversion he stated that he received a mighty baptism of the Holy Spirit and fire and "fairly bellowed the unspeakable overflow of my heart!"[1] As it was for the Moravians, God's visitation to Finney was dramatically powerful, and the results equally so. The Gospel spread and people were converted to Christ. I began to notice numerous such awakenings throughout history until I experienced my own.

Seeking the Holy Spirit

I draw a number of lessons from the New Testament and from more recent accounts about praying in the Spirit. We must believe the biblical record and the command of our Lord. We must be willing to tarry if necessary and wait on the Holy Spirit. We are not to seek manifestations but God Himself. We must get

1. Helen Wessel, ed. *The Autobiography of Charles G. Finney* (Minneapolis: Bethany House, 1977), 22.

into the Holy Spirit's presence before being filled with the Holy Spirit's power. When we sense His presence and power, we must yield to Him in faith.

Jesus said, "If anyone thirsts, let him come to Me and drink. . . . Out of his heart will flow rivers of living water" (John 7:37–38). He was speaking of the Holy Spirit. Notice the requirements: thirst—this is not for the satisfied. Come to Jesus—not to another source. Drink—receiving into oneself continuously. The overflow is abundant, continuous and from the heart, not the brain.

We get into the Holy Spirit in order to be filled with the Holy Spirit. I do not pray for someone to be filled with the Holy Spirit until I know that they have trusted Jesus, they are thirsty, they believe the promise and I sense the presence of the Holy Spirit. When they are filled, there is an overflow of joy, peace and boldness. I am not the Baptizer, nor can I make this experience happen. Jesus is, and He decides when and how; I am just the intercessor. But I have seen Him do it many, many times.

Praying in the Spirit is quite different from praying with the understanding. We should of course do both, but "in the Spirit" is a whole different realm (see 1 Corinthians 14:15). Praying in the Spirit increases our understanding as we study and meditate on Scripture. When we pray in the Spirit, the understanding is unfruitful, but in the Spirit we speak mysteries to God (see 1 Corinthians 14:2, 14).

I believe that the primary purpose of praying in the Spirit is personal devotion, not for public display. Paul makes it clear that our purpose in the Church is to build up others, not ourselves, by using understandable language (see 1 Corinthians 14:6–13). I can pray in the Spirit privately or quietly in the congregation and prophesy if the Lord gives me a word for the people. Prophecy is a succinct and distinct message, but that is a topic for a whole different book. (*Your Sons and Daughters Shall Prophesy*, by Ernest Gentile, is a good one.)

When we do not know how we should pray, we can allow the Spirit to help us (see Romans 8:26). He knows the mind of God (see 1 Corinthians 2:7–16). We can enter into the presence of the Holy Spirit because we have been counted righteous by faith in the blood of Christ. We can be filled with the Spirit and pray in the Spirit, who reveals to us the things of God that we have not seen or heard before, things that overcome the kingdom of darkness. Then our understanding is increased.

We can also pray in cooperation with the Holy Spirit. We can speak to God as before, but now we have sensitivity to Him as we speak. He can lead us to pray, in how to pray and in what to ask for. He keeps our prayer lives and our lives on track (see Acts 16:6–10). The Christian life was not meant to be lived separated from the presence, power and guidance of the Holy Spirit any more than Jesus intended that for His disciples. The Holy Spirit's power and guidance are absolutely necessary to following Jesus, who was also filled with the Holy Spirit.

Jesus was and is the door into a different realm, the realm of the Holy Spirit. Do I believe that every born-again child of God has the Holy Spirit within? Of course I do; that is how we know His voice and understand His Word. But is every child of God filled with the Spirit? Have all been baptized in the Holy Spirit and fire? Evidently not. Whatever terms one uses, I believe that we must seek the promise of the Father that Jesus Himself referred to as "baptism with the Holy Spirit" (see Acts 1:4–5; 11:16). John the Baptist said that Jesus would baptize with the Holy Spirit and fire. The issue is not to debate terms but to be filled with the Holy Spirit. It is a command.

It was the apostle Paul who implored Christians to "be filled with the Spirit" (Ephesians 5:18). Apparently some were not truly Spirit-filled Christians. Whatever terms we may use, Spirit-filled believers should not argue but allow room for the Lord's work in each one of us.

Dad's Wisdom

My father was a Spirit-filled minister. Shortly after I experienced the baptism of the Spirit, he offered very sound advice. "Charles, you just got into the spiritual realm a few days ago. I don't know how, but you did. Since I'm your father, can I give you some advice?"

"Yes, sir," I replied.

"You are just beginning; your enemy has been there since before the world was created. Just don't get to thinking you know a whole lot, you hear?"

"Yes, sir." I was properly warned and humbled.

We need to be aware that the Holy Spirit alone is able to safely guide us through the unknown and precarious world to the very throne of God. In terms of position, in God's eyes and grace, we are there. But experientially, we are here and need the Helper. The Bible is very clear in cautioning us against false spirits and unscriptural practices. The spiritual world is no playground (see Deuteronomy 18:9–14). That is one reason that we pray in Jesus' name, in His Spirit and according to His Word. There are many "channels" to avoid, and only one to pursue.

Whatever one believes it means to pray in the Holy Spirit, we should consider Jude 20: "But you, beloved, building yourselves up on your most holy faith, praying in the Holy Spirit." He alone knows the perfect will of God and can give us the power to perform it.

An Amazing Visit

After my experience and our church renewal, our denomination formed a "fellowship committee" to examine the church and me. I prayed a lot in the Holy Spirit during that season. I also traveled a lot, giving my own testimony, and I became known in numerous places. That in turn put pressure on our local association to do something about me.

On one occasion I was invited to speak to a small group of students in a house meeting in another city. They suggested that, while I was in town, I visit the local seminary and talk with a certain professor, whom I had heard before but did not know personally. I did not care for him because he had berated fundamentalists, when I was one. Then another person who heard about my trip made the same suggestion. I took it to mean that I should look up the professor.

I was completely unfamiliar with and unknown in that seminary when I walked into the administration building to inquire how I might meet the professor. Shortly after entering the building, I came face-to-face with him! I was caught off-guard, but I quickly introduced myself and told him my business: "I am here to talk with you about the baptism with the Holy Spirit and spiritual gifts." I expected an appointment later; instead he said, "Wait a moment. I'll get my mail." He quickly returned, canceled his class and gave me more than an hour. I was amazed!

As our conversation concluded, he said, "I don't know why you came to me, but many years ago, my brother received this experience. I was in the room with him when it came. I believe that it's real." I left appreciating his words and attitude, and I assumed that was all the Lord had in mind. That was in the spring.

In the fall, the denominational fellowship committee recommended to the association that our church be "disfellowshiped." After a long discussion, the pastor of the largest church in our area got up and said, "Where do we get off removing this church from our fellowship? We ought to call this committee the 'disfellowship committee.' Where did Paul say to remove a church because they believe in the gifts of the Holy Spirit? The Corinthian church certainly believed. Did Paul tell the Ephesian church to disfellowship the Corinthian church? In fact, the apostle Paul himself couldn't be a member of this association because he spoke in tongues more than all of them!" (See 1 Corinthians 14:18.)

You could hear a pin drop. We were not disfellowshiped. In fact, the pastor who spoke on our behalf was later elected to our association's highest office. What had just happened? I later learned that he had sought out a seminary professor to discuss the situation. Out of six denominational seminaries and hundreds of professors in our area, he had called the only one I had given my testimony to. A coincidence? No. I could give several other equally dramatic stories.

None of us know the future, but we can know the Lord and His Spirit. We can pray in the Holy Spirit, and He who does know the future will prepare us. That is vital. I hear lots of scenarios and prophecies about the future of our nation and world events. My counsel is to be watchful and study Scripture. Beyond that, pray diligently in the Spirit and trust Him to prepare us; to this end I strongly suggest reading 1 Peter 1. In the next chapter of this book, we will discuss what it means to pray fervently.

―――――― Discussion Questions ――――――

1. What do you believe it means to "pray in the Holy Spirit"?

2. Why do we need His help in our prayers?

3. What are the benefits of praying in the Spirit?

4. What is "cessationism"? Have you been exposed to it?

5. What verses promise us the apostolic experience?

6. Why is there controversy about what this means?

7. How can we protect ourselves from other spirits that would deceive us?

9

What Does It Mean
to Pray Fervently?

"The effective, fervent prayer of a righteous man avails much"
(James 5:16). In other words, there are great rewards to fervent
praying. What does it mean to pray fervently?

We are often driven to pray by some situation, relationship
or need that is motivating us to seek the Lord. The fervency of
our prayers will be, or should be, determined by the seriousness
of the need. Casual praying about a serious situation makes no
sense and is unlikely to yield results.

In addition to the rewards we might reap from fervent prayer,
the situation that drives us to God can also drive us to hear what
the Lord is saying to us, bringing necessary change in our own
lives. If we are serious, we will adjust to His will. Not so with
casual prayer. Fervent prayer leads us to first engage in God's
business in our own lives and then His business in the world,
as our will becomes engulfed in His.

I used to think that real prayer meant you had to weep, because I often heard my parents weep when they prayed about

family, finances, church life or people who did not know Jesus. They were serious about prayer, and their prayers got results.

Prayers That Get Results

When I was five years old, we left our home in the bayous to live in a basement apartment of a church in New Orleans, though we still made trips to the bayous where Dad ministered and stayed in touch with Mom's family. Then Dad got a call to pastor a very small church in south Alabama, one hundred fifty miles away. This was during World War II, and rationing of all kinds was in effect. Every fourth Sunday, Dad would take the Greyhound bus to the small community, stay in someone's home, visit the various families on foot, preach and then return to New Orleans.

Mom and I stayed behind, and I would spend a lot of time in the church basement because Mom was concerned for me on the city streets. We were also worried about the war, which felt very close. The city held air raid rehearsals, and on signal all the lights in the city had to go out. We would sit next to our large cabinet radio by the light of its small dial and listen to the news. A German submarine had sunk a ship off the mouth of the Mississippi River, and Pearl Harbor was a recent experience. Mom was only 24. I remember her prayers.

In a little over a year, we moved to south Alabama; the church was now large enough for my dad to go full-time. It was rural but more populated than the bayous had been, and the new community was Baptist. Mom still had some of her Cajun accent and had grown up Catholic. The small community in which she grew up could not afford a school with more than seven grades. The new church in Alabama had several teachers and the local school principal as members. Mom completed her GED while she was learning to be a Baptist pastor's wife; this was a large transition that called for tears and prayer.

The new community was kind, and our family moved into a "pastorium" next to the church's small, white chapel. (A pastorium is like an aquarium, except they keep preachers in it.) But it was a step up from the church basement. The community gave us a "pounding," which is a nice welcome in which everyone brings a pound of something: food, chickens and things to help get us started. One farmer brought us his favorite milk cow, and soon we had a pig, a garden and the necessities of life. Soon after that, the Lord added to our family with a sister and then a brother for me. This was very different from my bayou memories, but they were nevertheless good times.

The church continued to grow with its challenges and triumphs, and my parents continued to pray, often in tears. The church bought land, built buildings, bought more land and built more buildings; one building, which stood beside the highway, was a beautiful Gothic auditorium built of Tennessee Crab Orchard stone. I was old enough at this point to work alongside Dad and the other men in the community to help with the construction.

The church had never had a pastor that stayed long, but Dad was there for 35 years. It became the largest rural church in the county. His fellow ministers honored Dad in many ways. Even so, I do not know if this community that respected Dad so much ever really understood the fervent love and prayers that watered the growth. After Dad retired, the next pastor lasted one year.

The Truth Catches Up

I began in ministry not long after turning eighteen. I had been born in April, born again in another April, and responded to the call to be a minister in yet another April. The years just prior to eighteen were not ones in which I emulated my parents' prayer lives. I was engaged in sports, girls, drag racing and an occasional fight, trying to overcome being a preacher's kid. I was also smoking

king-size Pall Malls and sporting a ducktail haircut. My transition into ministry was not smooth. My prayer life had to be renewed.

When I began to pastor at age twenty, I had my parents' example of prayer, but I was "too cool" and self-reliant to do what they did. The church that I pastored also grew, mostly through hard work and God's grace, as I commuted first to college a hundred miles away and then to seminary in New Orleans, a hundred fifty miles away. Yet my prayer roots kept haunting me to seek God. The truth travels behind us sometimes, but it catches up eventually. After seven years of pastoring, the truth about me caught up. I had to get fervent with God in prayer again or quit the ministry.

Fervent is beyond—far beyond—casual. It is warmhearted, honest and even desperate. You cannot feign "fervent" with God. At least three things cause your prayers to become fervent: seeing the reality of your situation before God, realizing in your heart that you care and understanding that God cares. That removes a casual approach to God as you understand that all of life is in His hands. Casualness in such times produces casualties.

Fervency, like all that has to do with God, comes from the heart, and God searches the heart to uncover our motives, sin and calling (see 2 Chronicles 16:9; Jeremiah 17:10). The heart remains a mystery to me. Only God can show us what is truly in our hearts, to the deepest recesses, and He is the "consummate cardiologist." We get serious when He begins to show us that what is there is not pretty (see Jeremiah 17:9). The good news is that His motive toward us is goodness and mercy. He wants us to ask for a new heart.

A New Heart

I have read stories about people who have received a physical heart transplant and discovered changes in their appetites and attitudes. Is there more to the physical heart than a blood-pumping organ? In a spiritual sense, God can give us a "heart transplant," a new heart, a new creation. David is an example: He committed grievous and terrible sins such as adultery and even causing the death of a loyal and trusting soldier. David's sins cost his family and his nation, leading him to pray, "Create in me a clean heart . . ." (Psalm 51:10). The God who created also re-creates, as He did in David and millions of others.

The heart is the center of our being, the deepest recesses of the soul, the seat of our will, intellect and emotions. It is the spring from which all of life flows (see Proverbs 4:23). If the heart is pure, then life is pure; words are sincere and full of faith. If the heart is corrupt, then life is polluted.

Fervent prayer deals with our hearts before it deals with our lives. We must repent from the heart, believe in our hearts, confess with our mouths from our hearts and forgive from the heart. God can handle our sin if we honestly face it and repent; what He cannot handle is lukewarmness. It nauseates Him (see Revelation 3:14–19). He is passionate about us and wants us to respond in kind. Prayer must be about more than form, and it must proceed from passion in order to be effective (see 2 Timothy 3:5).

People with Heart

Jesus demonstrated righteous passion: He leaped for joy upon hearing the good reports of His followers. He wept over Jerusalem. He sweat blood in Gethsemane. He prayed all night. He was decisive and stood up to corrupt leaders. He had *heart*. Dying for others with a broken heart is as fervent as it gets. He saw what was coming to Israel and gave His all to warn them, forgive them and deliver them from it.

Samuel almost anointed Eliab, oldest of Jesse's sons, because he looked the part, but God rejected him because he lacked heart. David, on the other hand, would fight a lion, a bear or even a giant. He had heart.

One of my favorite individuals from history is Winston Churchill, who understood Hitler's evil nature long before others did. Neville Chamberlain, who served as British prime minister before Churchill, was naïve and passive, believing Hitler's word. All of Britain rejected Churchill's warnings and leadership, sending this statesman who understood the times into deep depression. When the war did come, Britain chose Churchill to lead, and he continually inspired his nation, as well as the United States, while it lasted. At the end of the war, Churchill said, "I was not the lion, but it fell to me to give the lion's roar."[1] As I look at the Church, I have to ask, "Where is the roar?"

It seems to me that much of the Church has had a "passion-ectomy," choosing comfort over conflict, politics over passion and form over fire. We have been anesthetized by self-interest and entertainment and evangelized by the postmodern culture. Many have become dependents deprived of their heritage; like Samson, our hair is shorn. We are often more like Chamberlain than Churchill.

Scripture is full of the accounts of people with heart, who serve as models for us:

> In spite of Samson's faults, no one could accuse him of lacking passion. He killed a thousand Philistines with the fresh jawbone of a donkey. Though captured and blinded by his enemies, who exploited his weakness for women, he still begged for the strength to pull down the temple of Dagon with his own hands. He loved not his own life unto death. In so doing, he killed more of the enemy in death than he had in life.

> Jacob's wife Rachel was so zealous to have children of her own that she cried from her heart, "Give me children or

1. John Antonakis, Anna T. Cianciolo, and Robert J. Sternberg, eds., *The Nature of Leadership* (Thousand Oaks, Calif.: Sage, 2004), 332.

I die!" God gave her two sons, but she died giving birth to the second.

Hannah, also aching for a son, prayed so fervently that the priest in the Tabernacle thought she was drunk. She later received that son, Samuel, and gave him to God.

A Canaanite woman turned to Jesus on behalf of her daughter, crying, "Have mercy on me, O Lord, Son of David! My daughter is severely demon-possessed." The disciples tried to drive her away, but because of her love for her daughter and faith in Jesus, she would not retreat. Her daughter was delivered (Matthew 15:21–28).

A blind man, Bartimaeus, refused to stay silent when Jesus passed by: "Jesus, Son of David, have mercy on me!" When others told him to be quiet, he only called louder. He was healed (Mark 10:46–52).

Get Serious

We are called not merely to know these stories or sing about them; we are called to live them. When issues are serious, we must get serious. This is not a "fanaticism" that has lost control; it is fervency borne of seeing reality. Ambivalence, delay or passivity in the face of danger is the door to disaster. Once evil enters the house, it may be too late to take a stand. We are here because of courage, vigilance and passion—because many who preceded us went out to meet the enemy, not waiting for him to come in.

This is the attitude exhibited by George Patton, United States general during World War II and the country's greatest tank commander. He accomplished amazing feats in warfare. Patton referred to foxholes as "graves," and he would not "dig in." He was always on offense: "When in doubt, attack!"[2]

2. Porter B. Williamson, *Patton's Principles* (Tucson: Management and Systems Consultants, Inc., 1979), 130.

Jesus said concerning the Church, "The gates of hell will not prevail against it." The Church was built to attack hell, not dig beautiful, state-of-the-art "foxholes." Prayer is where the assault against hell begins.

The word *courage* comes from the French word *coeur*, which means "heart." Churchill said, "Courage is rightly esteemed the first of human qualities . . . because it is the quality which guarantees all others."[3] Sweet courage! It is the ability to face difficulty and danger without fear of failure. It is a gift that comes from God to those who care more about a particular purpose and its rewards than they care about their very lives. Courageous people may often err, but the greater error is a lukewarm heart in the face of grave danger while God is watching (see Ezekiel 22:30).

Courage That Changes History

Another favorite story of mine is found in 1 Samuel 14. Jonathan, son of King Saul, and his armor bearer had left the camp of Saul's faltering army. They climbed a hill and prepared to attack a larger group of the enemy. When Jonathan explained his plan to the armor bearer, the armor bearer said, "Do all that is in your heart . . . I am with you." They won a great victory and inspired others with their courage. Every leader needs an armor bearer.

When Jesus was tried, beaten and mocked, a lot of people present knew it was wrong but remained silent, intimidated by the mob. They were passive in the face of humanity's worst decision ever. Even Pontius Pilate, who presided over the trial, knew Jesus was innocent, but he was still intimidated. His wife had warned him. He even tried to "wash his hands." Somewhere in hell, he is likely still trying to get the blood of Jesus off his

3. Stephen Mansfield, *Never Give In* (Nashville: Cumberland House Publishing, 2000), 94.

hands and protesting his plight. But the blood will not come off. Passivity is the mother of defeat.

Analysis is good and necessary, but when analysis transitions to delay fueled by fear, it becomes paralysis, like the possum that plays dead, hoping its adversary will go away. The most and best knowledge is of little value until it is applied in the arena of conflict. The greatest theology is of little value until lived. Luther was a great theologian, but we would never have heard of him if he had not taken a stand. Pope John Paul II was admired by much of the world because he went back to Poland and took a stand that began to unravel the Communist empire.

Serious opposition cannot be defeated by a casual response. Evil terrorists who would fly a planeload of innocent passengers into a tower, killing themselves, are serious. Demons who motivate somebody to shoot many people in a theater, a school, a mall or temple are serious. Natural and spiritual wars are both serious. The enemy is not out to injure us but to destroy us. It is time for God's people to become fervent. We need a change of heart, focus and commitment, and we need God's own courage. That is how we should pray!

Rewards of the Heart

Among my favorite Bible verses are Psalm 126:5–6.

> Those who sow in tears
> Shall reap in joy.
> He who continually goes forth weeping,
> Bearing seed for sowing,
> Shall doubtless come again with rejoicing,
> Bringing his sheaves with him.

The rewards of fervent prayer are as numerous as the requests that we bring to God: a good marriage and family, righteous children, strong churches, salvation, success, a strong and righteous nation, powerful missions here and abroad and fulfillment of Jesus' prophecy: "This gospel of the kingdom will be preached in all the world" (Matthew 24:14).

When you kneel to pray, consider yourself seated "in Christ" at the Father's right hand, travailing with Him over His strategy in the earth. He has given you a place in His plan and works with you to fulfill it. He has put names and places on your heart to be affected by His power as you cooperate with Him. He is serious about His will, and when we are serious, we will see it done on earth as it is in heaven. This is our opportunity to reap and rejoice with Him.

Sometimes we allow ourselves a false comfort fostered by a "lullaby theology," ignoring the by-and-by danger. We make alibis, turn over in our beds of ease and sleep like Rip van Winkle. There are no crowns for the complacent, no gold medals for spectators. We cannot earn our salvation, but we can be found worthy heirs of it by the courageous fervency that was His and can be ours. If not, our children will one day lament our failure. If we arise, they will one day count us among the faithful, and that would be one great reward.

I have not mentioned what the Lord Himself might do or say when we meet Him, but "Well done!" would be more than enough! Let us consider what it means to "labor in prayer" and receive His "Well done." Labor is essential to reaping a harvest.

—————— Discussion Questions ——————

1. Can you recall times when you prayed fervently?

2. What does fervent praying mean to you?

3. Can you cite several biblical examples of fervent prayer?

4. How do we know that God's love for us is fervent?

5. Do you believe that God's choice of a person for a specific role has something to do with his or her passion?

6. Do you think that we, like Samuel, get fooled by appearance? Have you been fooled?

7. What are some issues about which we should now pray fervently?

10

Is Prayer Worth the Labor?

A woman, when she is in labor, has sorrow because her hour
has come; but as soon as she has given birth to the child, she
no longer remembers the anguish, for joy that a human being
has been born into the world.

John 16:21

Every mother understands this verse. Giving birth is a labor of
love from a mother to a child. As a husband and father, I have
watched both the labor and the joy; it is an amazing process that
deserves our deep gratitude toward the mother who endures it.

Every reward is the result of someone's labor. That is the way
life works; nothing of great value comes without a price. This
is certainly true of prayer.

As I stated in the previous chapter, among my favorite verses
are Psalm 126:5–6:

> Those who sow in tears
> Shall reap in joy.
> He who continually goes forth weeping,

Bearing seed for sowing,
Shall doubtless come again with rejoicing,
Bringing his sheaves with him.

I grew up in a farming community and benefited from my father's belief in hard work, though I was not always happy about it. I learned that farming was difficult; I had to wake early and work hard to enjoy the rewards of the harvest. In order to enjoy our labor, we must keep the rewards in mind (see Hebrews 12:2). If we lose sight of the reward, labor becomes more difficult, even depressing.

Creation itself was a labor, as God worked six days before resting on the seventh. According to natural and spiritual law, we too must labor to enter rest (see Hebrews 4:4–11). According to the book of Ecclesiastes, man's greatest blessing is to enjoy his labor (see Ecclesiastes 5:18–20). Many suffer the great tragedy of seeing little or no meaning in their work and cannot enjoy the fruits of their labor. Such people would do well to learn to labor in prayer in order to see greater rewards from the One who rewards us faithfully.

We often enjoy the fruits of others' prayers—our historical heroes, parents and pastors—while being unwilling to labor in prayer ourselves. Laziness in prayer assures that the harvest we want will soon disappear. Entertainment, self-indulgence and apathy bring their own harvest, albeit not an enduring, joyful one. We must realize that all that we love and appreciate has come from the sweat and tears of diligent labor. But the labor of the past will not produce the harvest of the future. Scripture is clear: If we refuse to labor, there will be no harvest (see Proverbs 21:25, 31).

Even when we work hard, we are dependent on the favor of God. "Unless the LORD builds the house, they labor in vain who build it; unless the LORD guards the city, the watchman stays awake in vain" (Psalm 127:1). Just as farmers understand that they need rain at the right time or the crops will dry up, labor in prayer begins when we realize that our best effort is not enough—we are still dependent on the Lord. If we love our cities and we love the harvest, we will labor in prayer to seek the Lord's help.

Wrestling in Prayer

My friend Gregory Mira was a wrestler in high school. He describes facing an opponent this way: "It's not a team sport, just you and the opponent in the ring struggling to overcome and win the prize. Grappling, holding fast, casting down the opponent is excruciating, muscle-numbing work."

We wrestle for a much greater prize: that which God has placed in our hearts. The apostle Paul likened our battle with the enemy to a wrestling match: "For we do not wrestle against flesh and blood, but against principalities, against powers, against the rulers of the darkness of this age, against spiritual hosts of wickedness in the heavenly places" (Ephesians 6:12).

Often we are not wrestling with a spiritual enemy; we are wrestling with our own nature, which the enemy is using against us. Sometimes we even wrestle with the Lord Himself; such was the case with Jacob in Genesis 32:24. After years working for his treacherous uncle Laban, Jacob returned to his own country to meet his older brother, whom Jacob had cheated out of his inheritance. Esau, hearing of Jacob's return, came to meet Jacob with a formidable force. To appease his angry brother, Jacob sent his family and possessions ahead as offerings while he stayed behind to wrestle with God. He did so all night; he would not let go without the Lord's blessing.

In the end God did bless him, changed his name and nature and gave him favor with Esau. Jacob's battle was not with Esau; it was with God. This relates to us as well. Before we confront the enemy, we must wrestle God and our very selves. True repentance and humility are not easy; they often come with tears and time alone with God.

Prior to his conversion, the apostle Paul wrestled with God without realizing it. God had been "goading" him. Finally, on the Damascus road, God knocked him down hard and blinded him (see Acts 9). Paul had thought he was wrestling against Christians, but in fact he was wrestling with the Lord Himself. Paul surrendered, obeyed and was healed and filled with the Holy Spirit. He became a champion wrestler in a different arena.

Paul became a laborer in prayer, striving according to God's working in him (see Colossians 1:29). He was persecuted, hard pressed and perplexed, daily dying to himself and ultimately being martyred. But he was an overcomer in all of these areas. He also produced others who could labor in prayer, like Epaphras, Timothy and Titus. He and Silas labored in prayer and praise in the Philippian jail until the Lord shook the building and saved the jailer; this began a church (see Acts 16:16–34). Theirs were not mere formal petitions for protection; they were jail-breaking prayers of labor and faith.

We cannot impart what we do not practice; methods alone will not bring such amazing results. It is easy for me to review my life and ministry and see the fruits of laboring in prayer and the sad results of failing to do so. I can preach prayer, but I cannot impart it unless I am doing it. Praying in the past was good, but continuing prayer alone will secure the future and call others to engage in it. I can "preach" measles, but if I have the mumps, that's what they'll get!

Pray for Laborers

Jesus said to pray for laborers to enter the harvest, because the harvest was great and the laborers few (see Matthew 9:36–38).

We must be willing to endure the pains of labor if we are to see new births added to the family of God. The harvest can be reaped if we labor in prayer to the "Lord of the harvest" for laborers—people willing to work for it. There are few things sadder than to see a crop dying in the fields for lack of workers. All of the preparation and rewards are lost. The crop is ready now; are we ready to labor for those who need Jesus Christ?

Laboring in prayer is more effective than "pushing" people toward Him. My wife was an exceptional lady, kind, supportive and quiet in her spirit. She loved family and children and supported me unreservedly in all that I did. She laughed at my jokes and encouraged me in my work. Carolyn was a gift from God. My temperament was difficult, and sometimes I am sure it was embarrassing, even though she never said it. My own needs, not hers, drove me to God.

After my renewal, I wanted her to be blessed in the same way, but she was not as needy as I was. The Lord prompted me to change myself without trying to change her. Some around us wanted her to manifest more "spirituality." (Dealing with the expectations and demands of others is an experience most pastors' wives understand.) Some showed their desire for her to be "more spiritual" in aggressive ways; I objected, as this simply drove her away. She was kind and sensitive, but she had her own convictions, which were deeply held.

The Lord had simply told me to pray for her diligently, and I did. I did not pray for her because I saw changes she needed to make; I prayed for her because I wanted her to experience joy and peace. But most of all, I prayed because I loved her. Two years later the Lord graciously filled her with His Spirit and gave her a new joy. Being my wife, and a pastor's wife, had brought her great stress.

After the Lord blessed her, I asked, "What made you seek the Lord to be filled with His Spirit?" She smiled and said, "I saw the change in you and wanted that too, but I wanted to see if it would last."

We need to labor in prayer—not only for others, but so that our growth in the Lord will endure and increase. Maybe people in the world are watching and waiting, asking the same question Carolyn asked: Will it last?

The Intercessor's Reward

I have been blessed by "prayer warriors" that have been faithful in all seasons. Not only did they tell me that they were praying for me daily, I have felt their prayers. There is no doubt in my mind that I owe a great debt to them.

The enemy knows that if he can knock out the shepherd, the flock will be destroyed. Pastors and all leaders are special targets. They need intercessors who are willing to labor in prayer for their leaders (see Hebrews 13:7, 17). If pastors and leaders had as many intercessors as critics, the world would be a better place.

My friend R.T. Pickens was a quiet man who loved the Lord and loved to pray; he is with the Lord now. R.T. was a carpenter and homebuilder who was sensitive to the Holy Spirit. In my darkest hours of ministry, R.T. would come by the office to pray with me. He often shed tears as he labored on my behalf. When we rose from our knees, he would smile, his eyes still wet, and say, "It will be all right." And it was.

Several years ago I had open-heart surgery—a quadruple bypass. I had just a 10 percent blood supply, and the doctor warned that if I had a heart attack, I would die. Naturally, others joined me in praying. My greatest comfort came from the word I heard from Jesus: *I am praying for you.* I had peace through the entire ordeal.

Only God knows the entire list of people willing to labor in prayer for each of us, but it is not overstating the case to say we are here because they cared enough. Whether it is George Washington kneeling in the snow at Valley Forge or a grandmother kneeling by her bed, we have been the reward of their prayers.

How great are the rewards of our labor in prayer? Are they worth sowing in tears and laboring to enter God's rest through prayer? Do you believe Hebrews 11:6, that He rewards those who *diligently* seek Him? Do you believe that the Lord sent fire and rain as a result of Elijah's prayers? Is Jesus the same yesterday, today and forever? Is anything too hard for God? And, perhaps most significantly, how much do you want His reward?

A good husband or wife is a great reward. One day a single friend told me, "I don't believe that there are any more good women." I asked him, "Where are you looking?" He named all the clubs that he was visiting. I suggested that maybe he was looking for love in all the wrong places. Finally he turned to the Lord and was given a wonderful wife. I performed their marriage ceremony.

A son or daughter who makes you proud is another great reward (see Proverbs 27:11). Matthew 11:19 tells us that wisdom is justified by her children. When we labor in prayer for our children, teaching them God's Word, seeing them emerge as godly children is a great reward.

A Mighty Visitation

Many years ago I heard an account of the great revival in the Hebrides Islands off the coast of Scotland. Peggy and Christine Smith, sisters aged 82 and 84 who were residents of the Hebrides, began to pray about their dwindling church. Peggy was blind and Christine was extremely arthritic, so they could not attend church. Nevertheless they began praying a promise of Scripture: "I will pour water on him who is thirsty, and floods on the dry ground" (Isaiah 44:3). In 1949 the Lord revealed to Peggy that revival was coming and that the church of their fathers would be crowded with young people. She told the pastor to prepare for revival.

In the same district a group of church leaders were praying in a barn. A young deacon arose and read Psalm 24:3–5:

> Who may ascend into the hill of the LORD? Or who may stand in His holy place? He who has clean hands and a pure heart, who has not lifted up his soul to an idol, nor sworn deceitfully. He shall receive blessing from the LORD, and righteousness from the God of his salvation.

The deacon said, "Brethren, it seems to me just so much 'humbug'; to be waiting and praying as we are, if we ourselves are not rightly related to God." Then, lifting his hands toward heaven, he cried, "Oh God, are my hands clean? Is my heart pure?" God's presence filled the barn and God's power was loosed in their lives. A great revival came to the islands as thousands met Jesus. Young people piled into the churches.

The stories about the rewards mean little until we become thirsty and willing to labor in prayer. Are we there yet? I pray so; the dangers are all around us, but the reward is just ahead. Sow in tears and reap with joyful shouting so that we can testify among the nations, "The Lord has done great things for us, and we are glad" (Psalm 126:3). That will be worth the labor!

Now let us move to the subject of righteousness. We must ask ourselves, as the young deacon did, "Is my heart pure? Are my hands clean?"

Discussion Questions

1. Why is prayer sometimes difficult?

2. Have there been times when you labored in prayer? Have you labored for non-Christians?

3. Have you experienced breakthroughs in prayer?

4. What are some issues in your life that require laboring in prayer?

5. Do you believe that the Lord is calling you to more serious prayer?

6. If so, in what ways can you respond?

7. Are the rewards worth the labor?

11

How Does Righteousness Affect Our Prayers?

Can our righteousness change how effective our prayers are? This is an interesting and important question. Elijah was called a righteous man whose prayer was effective. Yet he was also a man subject to the same passions we are. Certainly he was not righteous due to his own works (see Romans 3:10, 23). Yet he is counted righteous by his faith in God and his obedience to God. He was a just and impartial man (see Habakkuk 2:4; James 2:1–9).

When we pray, we should realize two things: The Lord counts us righteous before Him once we accept that Jesus died in our place to take our sins upon Himself (see Isaiah 53). Next we must realize that Jesus wants us to become what He already counts us to be. This happens as we fellowship with Him in His Word and Spirit, and obey. Being counted righteous is an immediate transaction; becoming righteous is a journey.

Prayer is the path to beholding Him and being changed into His image (see 2 Corinthians 3:17–18). While He loves us as we are, He loves us too much to leave us the way we are. What He counts us to be He will make us to be—righteous. Righteousness is simply right: right with Him, our loved ones, our fellow Christians and our neighbors. This is the whole law (see Mark 12:28–33).

James addresses why prayers are not heard in James 4:3: "You ask and do not receive, because you ask amiss, that you may spend it on your pleasures." Self-centeredness is not righteous. James continues to address sin in the lives of Christians: "God resists the proud, but gives grace to the humble" (James 4:6). Both James and John stress confessing our faults, confessing sins and acting with humility before God and one another. Dealing with our issues is humbling but cleansing.

David wrote from experience in Psalm 66:18, "If I regard iniquity in my heart, the Lord will not hear." Iniquity is "inequity": perverse dealings, dishonesty, entertaining sin in one's heart.

The enemy knows this truth and exploits it; his plan is to seduce us, to beguile us in order to short-circuit our relationship with our Holy God. He wants to reduce our prayer lives to mere form without power (see 2 Timothy 3:5). He wants to take our focus off seeking God and move it to self-serving pleasure, and he has had a lot of success. The account of Balaam (Numbers 22–25) is a good example of how he works.

Balaam

On their journey from the flatlands of Egypt to the hills and mountains of Canaan, the Israelites camped near the land of Moab. The Moabites were alarmed because of the massive numbers of Israelites, who would daily consume tons of food. They were also afraid because the Israelites had already defeated the Amalekites.

The Moabites were an immoral and weak people, descendants of an incestuous relationship between Lot and his daughter (see

Genesis 19:30–38). Their king, Balak, was afraid, and he sent all the way to Mesopotamia for a known prophet, Balaam—who was not a prophet of God—to prophesy against Israel. The story is humorous but also tragic. The Lord told Balaam not to go, but as Balak's offers increased, Balaam decided to go anyway. On the way he had some trouble when the Lord appeared to his donkey. The donkey kept trying to get off of the path, on one occasion injuring Balaam. In his frustration Balaam even argued with the animal, who talked back to him! Finally the Lord appeared to Balaam and warned him.

When Balaam reached Moab, Balak showed him the encamped Israelites and urged him to prophesy against them to curse them. But each time that Balaam prophesied, he blessed them profusely instead. This of course irritated Balak. Finally Balaam and Balak gave up. But though he could not curse Israel, whom God had blessed, Balaam could give Balak the key to harming Israel: Invite the Israelite men to the grossly immoral feast of Baal, where they would be seduced by Moabite women. When the men of Israel sinned on their own accord, God would judge and punish them (see Numbers 31:16; Revelation 2:14). And that is just what Balak did.

The Moabites worshiped Baal and Astarte, god and goddess of fertility. Prostitution was part of their worship. As the Moabite women "introduced themselves" to the men of Israel, the men fell into sin, and God punished them (see Numbers 25:1; Micah 6:5; 2 Peter 2:15–16). If the enemy cannot curse us or defeat us, he will seek to join himself to us and bring on us the wages of unrighteousness. It is one thing to be opposed by Moab, quite another to be opposed by God. (As a warning to us, Balaam is mentioned in eight books of the Bible.)

Balaam was later killed, but not before he wreaked havoc on Israel. He could not curse them, but he could tell Balak how to seduce them. I am not afraid of the curses of the wicked, but I do fear the Lord. God is holy, and in order to fellowship with Him, He requires a life sanctified and separated from the worldly culture (see 1 Thessalonians 5:23; Hebrews 10:10). We must deal with the world; though we are not of it, we must go into it with the Gospel (see John 17; Acts 2:40). The key to successfully doing that is to stay before the Lord in prayer.

Confession

James tells us to confess our sins. Our Catholic friends seem to value confession more than those of us who are evangelical. Though I am a pastor, I also have a pastor, and I believe that we all should have a pastor. I trust this person and have practiced the deepest kind of confession with him (see John 20:23). When I do this, he gives me forgiveness and counsel. I believe that I have received the forgiveness and counsel of God. None of us are too elevated to humble ourselves; even the Pope has a "father confessor." Many a person would have been spared tragic results had they confessed early and often. It is the cover-up that kills. Accountability comes either early or late, but it always comes.

Confession builds a bond between the one who confesses and the one who receives confession. I have also received confession and highly value the confidence of the confessor. To betray that confidence would cause trouble with the Lord and others. I recommend confessing to someone if you know that there is an offense, confessing to God what you have done and confessing to someone that you really do trust. Hopefully your pastor is that person, but whoever it may be, we all need to cleanse our hearts through confession if our prayers are to be effective.

Thank God that the priesthood of Jesus is continual (see 1 John 1:7–10; Hebrews 7:25; 9:11–15; 10:19–22). If we confess, He is faithful to forgive and cleanse us from all unrighteousness. Indeed, the bond that exists between the one who confesses and the one who receives confession exists between us and Him. He made a covenant with us in His own blood; we can trust Him to hear our confession, knowing that He gave His life to forgive us. It also builds a bond when we confess our faults to one another; it demonstrates trust and forgiveness. The unwillingness to confess reveals pride and mistrust. It is not that the Lord or even others do not know what we have done; it is that they need to know that *we* know. Then they can forgive.

Rewards of Confession

James tells us that confession and righteousness are necessary to effectively praying for healing. Of course he is not referring to self-righteousness but to faith and obedience. Jesus said that those who hunger and thirst for righteousness would be filled—filled with righteousness and the rewards of it:

Seek first the kingdom of God and His righteousness, and all other good things will be added (see Matthew 6:33).

We need have no anxiety over the cares and needs of life that others worry about, and we will never have to beg (see Matthew 6:25).

We will not have to fear (see Proverbs 28:1); the Lord will uphold us (see Psalm 37:17–39).

We are positioned to receive favor with God and be fruitful (see Psalm 1:1–6).

We can have great joy, free of guilt and condemnation (see Psalm 68:3; Romans 14:17).

We can endure amid trials (see Proverbs 10).

The righteous are promised eternal life (see Matthew 25:46).

This is by no means a complete list, but I will add Proverbs 14:34: "Righteousness exalts a nation." We need to seek the Lord, who counts us righteous, and repent, confess our sins and pray for our nation (see Nehemiah 1:1–11; 2 Chronicles 7:14). We must see ourselves as part of the problem, the way Nehemiah did. We are to be "the light of the world," but perhaps our light has grown dim by division, pride and lack of repentance. Can we blame the world for acting like the world? The burden to seek His righteousness lies with us. Then His light will shine through us, and darkness cannot extinguish it.

Next we will examine the importance of praying according to the Word of God.

Discussion Questions

1. What did James mean when he said Elijah was like us?

2. What is imputed righteousness?

3. What is imparted righteousness?

4. Why is righteousness important to our prayers?

5. What is the enemy's strategy to defeat us?

6. What are some rewards of righteousness?

7. Why is confession important to righteousness?

12

Should I Quote Scripture When I Pray?

As I said earlier, I learned to pray hearing my parents pray. They would often pray by saying, "Lord, you said . . ." I instinctively believed that part of my prayer life should include what the Lord has said as it relates to my request. That meant knowing what He had said in the Bible, so I had to learn Scripture.

I grew up in a Bible-believing church. We did not always interpret the Bible correctly, but we did believe it. In fact, even before I knew much of it, I believed it to be the very Word of God—the *Holy* Bible. We studied it in Sunday school, heard it preached and studied it again in vacation Bible school. I knew more Bible stories as a child than most adults do. In vacation Bible school, the teachers gave us index cards with verses on them, and we received stars as we memorized those verses. To this day I still quote the King James Version by heart, though through the years I have used many other versions.

We had "sword drills": As we stood in a line across the front of the auditorium, the teacher called out a verse, and the first person to find it in the Bible stepped forward. Every child tried to learn where the books of the Bible were, and how many books were in each testament, in order to be first. I could go on, but you get the picture. We loved the Bible.

At home, we had a "promise box" on the table that contained numerous small cards, each containing a Bible promise. At each meal we would pull out a promise and read it. This was our normal way of life, and I thought it was normal for most people. "Your word I have hidden in my heart, that I might not sin against You" (Psalm 119:11). I did sin, all too often, but the Word was being hidden in my heart.

At age seventeen, I was in a statewide public speaking contest, and just prior to it, my father gave me a Bible marked up in various places in Proverbs. He seemed to know which verses I needed, since I was not walking with God in those days.

I will never forget my first encounter with a contradiction to the Bible; I was in an eighth-grade science class, and the subject was the theory of evolution. I was troubled, not because I accepted evolution but because the teacher was a good Christian and told us that she had to teach from the textbook. That was only the beginning—college and seminary came not long after. It seemed that every year the challenges to the Word of God became more intense. I was not one of those who cast aside my belief in the Bible; it was much too deep within. But I did react to and almost rejected the entire educational system, which I saw as anti-Bible and anti-God. As an adult I have witnessed the impact of secular education on the youth of America. Someone ought to ask, "How is that working out?"

The Foundation

Our confidence in the Bible as God's Word will have a great impact on how we pray, what we pray for and the results of our prayers. If we have confidence in His Word, then His Word should be the foundation of our prayers. Prayer is futile if we do not believe in the One to whom we speak. Believing in Him is the very essence of salvation and Christian life.

A strong foundation is key to walking in faith. Back in the early 1980s, I sent my son, who had recently graduated from college, to visit friends in Europe and the Middle East. He had traveled to those places with family before. In England he interviewed the editor of the London *Daily Telegraph*. The bishop of York had recently denied the virgin birth of Jesus and the resurrection, and then lightning struck his church. In the course of the interview, the editor asked, "Why would the bishop question the very basis of his own existence as a minister?" The editor was not a practicing Christian, but he got the question right.

Faith in God and His Word is the foundation of faith in our covenant God (see Deuteronomy 7:9). Every word that proceeds from His mouth is a covenant word; they are words Jesus Himself lived by and quoted (see Matthew 4:4). It is not my purpose here to argue the point or to state all of my reasons for believing in the original texts of the Bible. I will say that among the strongest reasons is that our Lord and the apostles believed it and quoted often from it (see 2 Timothy 3:14–17; 2 Peter 1:16–21).

The Apostles' Confidence

Romans 1:1–4 demonstrates the apostle Paul's confidence in the Old Covenant. He recognized Jesus as the One promised by the prophets in the Holy Scriptures. Paul calls Scripture "Holy," and his confidence in Jesus was scriptural, not merely emotional or based on "feelings" or circumstance. Confidence in Scripture supersedes our emotions and establishes us in all situations, even dangerous ones. Paul also passed on this confidence to his disciples, for example, by instructing Timothy to preach the Word in all seasons (see 2 Timothy 4:1–5). He also quoted the Old Testament extensively as the authority for his teachings—for example, in 1 Timothy 2:2 he refers to Ezra 6:10 to urge prayer for rulers.

So it has been my practice, like the Bereans of Acts 17:10–11, to search Scripture to see if what I hear is true. When confronted with the neoorthodox theology that was becoming popular in the 1950s and 1960s, I examined its content against the Word of God and found it lacking. Neoorthodoxy does to theology what a taxidermist does to a fish: It maintains form without life. There is no "new orthodoxy," just the settled Word of God.

When I hungered for a deeper experience with God, I did not search theology books, though some would have been useful; I searched the gospels, the epistles, Acts and the prophets. Joel in particular gave me confidence to ask God to pour His Spirit upon me. I prayed to be filled with the Holy Spirit based on Scripture.

Therefore, if we desire to pray about the vital issues of life, we must pray according to the Word of God—in faith. That faith comes from hearing the Word of God. Praying the Word in the Holy Spirit not only builds our faith for answered prayer, it enables us to know the will of God, which is stated in the Bible. We would not pray to steal something, or to get another man's wife. Why not? Because we know from Scripture that these are not the will of God. But we should pray for more character, love and power, and for the lost, because we know from Scripture these are the will of God (see Romans 5:1–5; 12:2; 1 Thessalonians 4:3).

The Lord Said

Another authentication of God's Word is that prophecies inspired by the Holy Spirit come to pass. This is true whether the prophecy is recorded in Scripture or spoken by an individual. I do not equate spoken prophecy with the Bible, but if a prophetic word comes to pass, we can know that it comes from God.

I was drawn to Ken Sumrall, my pastor, for many reasons, but principally because he had both a deep love for and knowledge of the Bible. When we prayed together, I often heard him say, as my parents had, "Lord, You said . . ." I had confidence in his prayers, and they were effective. He led a large church, a Bible college and a mission organization. But before all of that came to pass, he often prayed in agony, "Lord, You said . . ." We were bonded in a common love and faith in God and His Word.

One night, in the early days of our ministries, as we prayed with another prayer partner, the Lord came into the room with us. Each of us was fighting to survive opposition in our ministries, and our circumstances seemed threatening. There was no evidence of success as we paced back and forth in prayer across the room. Then the third member of our prayer group began to prophesy. "As you walk together in prayer, you will walk together in ministry around the world."

This seemed very unlikely, and at first I thought our friend had simply been "carried away" in the presence of God. But less than three years later, Ken and I boarded a plane for a ministry trip that literally took us around the world. The quality and accuracy of a prophetic word cries out for the utmost respect (Revelation 1:3; 19:10).

Knowing the Real

Praying the Word and will of God has many benefits: building faith, understanding the will of God and discerning what is not the will of God. As we get to know Scripture, we can know the real from the counterfeit. U.S. Treasury agents cannot know all the possible counterfeit versions of currency, but they are so acquainted with the real currency that they can soon spot a false product. We do not have to know all of the counterfeit, just the real.

We live in a time of gross spiritual and biblical ignorance. When I grew up in a small rural community, the Bible was read and prayers were offered prior to classes at school. The principal was a deacon in the church, and most teachers went to church. Some taught Sunday school. Of course this is no longer true, as we live in a "pluralistic society." While I respect those who believe differently and would defend their right to do so, I do not equate all beliefs and practices; that is foolish. God's Kingdom alone is unshakable and will stand forever (see Hebrews 12). But many are perishing for lack of knowledge.

Micah 6:8 says, "He has shown you, O man, what *is* good; and what does the LORD require of you but to do justly, to love mercy, and to walk humbly with your God?" In Psalm 119:92–94, it is written, "Unless Your law had been my delight, I would then have perished in my affliction. I will never forget Your precepts, for by them You have given me life. I am Yours, save me; for I have sought Your precepts."

My wife's grandmother, who lived to be almost 102, was among those who learned His precepts. She loved the Lord and His Word and memorized great portions of it. Often she shared something she saw in the Word, even in her old age. She was strong in faith and had a visitation from an angel just before, and the day of, her passing into glory. What a great legacy she left us. (I will share more of her story in the last chapter.)

I have trusted the Word of God and the God of His Word for more than sixty years at this writing. My parents before me did also. All three of our children serve God: One is a pastor, one is a missionary and the third serves our publishing ministry. My pastor trusted in the Word of God as does my family. We have sown and reaped.

When you pray the very words of God, you are stating your confidence in His covenant nature and His covenant words. Study the Word of God and pray the Word of God; then live the Word of God and enjoy the rewards of the Word of God. What are those rewards? Let me offer three out of a multitude that have shaped my own life:

- A kept heart brings life (see Proverbs 4:20–23).
- Faithfulness brings increase (see Luke 16:10–12).
- Sowing determines reaping (see Psalm 126:5–6).

What I have written is not merely a theory or doctrine. The Lord said in Malachi 3:10, "Try Me now in this. . . ." We have done this—to our satisfaction. He has proven to us that His Word is faithful and true (see Revelation 19:11).

In the next chapter we will examine what should happen once you offer up your prayers: hearing from God.

Discussion Questions

1. Have I settled in my heart that the Bible is God's Word?

2. Have I applied myself to diligently study the Bible?

3. Have I discovered God's will as taught in the Bible?

4. Am I praying about those things that the Bible tells us are God's will?

5. Describe some of God's will as revealed in the Bible.

6. Do I spend more time analyzing the Bible or applying it?

7. What are some of the rewards of applying biblical principles?

8. How can we know if a teaching is true?

13

Should I Expect to Hear from God?

When you pray, should you expect to hear from God? Absolutely yes. There have been times in my life when hearing from God made all the difference in the world; I will tell of just two. I waited several years for one answer, while the other came immediately.

In 1979 the United States Internal Revenue Service (IRS) initiated a five-year audit of our church, and we could not determine why. (In a five-year audit, the IRS examines every transaction for the past five years.) We answered questions and tried to cooperate, but we received no information as to why we were being investigated. We soon realized that we needed an attorney. The potential consequences of that kind of investigation could be severe to our church, our members and even other churches if bad precedents were established. As senior pastor, I carried a great burden.

Over the next three years, we hired additional attorneys and spent more than $100,000. Finally, on the advice of our attorneys, we sued the IRS based on the Freedom of Information Act. That is when we discovered that the IRS had documents and records stolen from our archives.

We suspected a former part-time secretary of stealing the documents and sending them to the IRS. The issue that triggered the audit was that a member had given a very large contribution that we later returned because the motives for the gift proved unacceptable. To the IRS, it appeared that we had been in collusion with the donor to help him avoid taxes. Of course that was not the case, and it could have been explained had we been given the opportunity. Meanwhile we endured great stress, loss of sleep and loss of resources.

After three years of this process, I attended a conference in another city. During one of the meetings the conference attendees were in a place of high worship, and the presence of God was evident. In that moment I lifted my heavy burden to the Lord, and then I heard Him speak to my spirit, *It is over!* It was clear and forceful. Peace and joy flooded my soul—I cannot describe the joy that I felt! I had not yet heard from the IRS, but I had heard from God! In a few weeks, the investigation was over and we were exonerated.

Following this ordeal, our church administrator, Michael Coleman, helped get a law passed through Congress, the Church Audit Procedures Act.

During those same three years, another event occurred that added to our stress. Three of my ministry colleagues were sued for millions of dollars by a famous psychiatrist who lived in California. The basis for his suit was a rumor that he had committed suicide. One of my colleagues repeated the rumor in a conference, and the message was broadcast over the radio in California, where such a comment was a legal offense. Under questioning, my friend said that he had heard the rumor from two other ministry friends of mine. So all three of them were sued for $40 million.

The psychiatrist hired a powerful and aggressive attorney who deposed the colleague who had repeated the rumor at the conference. The questioning lasted three days, during which the attorney made deprecating remarks about Jesus, calling Him a "penniless wanderer." The transcript of the deposition ran over five hundred pages, and the experience left my friend in tears. When I read it, I was furious. I was also asked to coordinate the defense for my other two ministry friends, even while I was still dealing with the IRS on behalf of our local church.

The psychiatrist's attorney was scheduled to come to our city next to depose the second friend who had repeated the rumor. I did two things: First, I instructed our attorney not to tolerate any deprecating remarks about our Lord. Second, I secluded myself in prayer. I realized as I prayed that I was in the presence of God, and He showed me that while my friends had erred, we were dealing with a spiritual force that was seeking to take advantage of and destroy ministries. I was led to bind that spirit, and I knew immediately that the Lord had heard me.

The opposing attorney did conduct the second deposition, but our attorney reported that he behaved in a professional and courteous manner. Though I cannot discuss the details for legal reasons, the suit was settled in an amicable and just manner, with a minor penalty.

Let me add that I was not the only one praying in either situation—many friends stood with us. Did we change God's mind? I do not think so; we just finally discovered what His mind was.

Forefathers Who Heard

The list of those who heard God both in the Bible and in history fills heaven's library. We who follow Jesus and our believing forefathers are now being called upon to pray, seek God and wait for His answer. We need His guidance and power in these critical times. Isaiah 55:11 reminds us that God performs His Word and accomplishes what He pleases. Going through life without hearing His voice is blindly walking into traffic without being able to hear.

Many situations in our personal lives, families, churches, communities and nation call for serious prayer. If we will not do it, who will? We are priests unto God, sanctified to intercede for others. We can avert tragedies and reap the rewards of effective prayers, and if we pray, Scripture tells us that He will show us great and mighty things that we do not yet know (see Jeremiah 33:3). But we need to hear Him and His will.

Habakkuk's prayer in Habakkuk 1 is an example of bold, honest praying and waiting to hear the results. Habakkuk and the Lord seemed to engage in a debate about violence and injustice, a debate that others want to have with the Lord as well. Then Habakkuk said,

> I will stand my watch and set myself on the rampart, and watch to see what He will say to me, and what I will answer when I am corrected. Then the LORD answered me and said: "Write the vision and make it plain on tablets, that he may run who reads it."
>
> Habakkuk 2:1–2

In verse 14 the Lord added, "For the earth will be filled with the knowledge of the glory of the LORD, as the waters cover the sea."

Habakkuk was boldly honest with God but open to correction. He also expected an answer. The Lord did answer and gave Habakkuk instructions to tell others plainly what he saw, and Habakkuk did as he was told. He saw that judgment would eventually come to the wicked, but that God would fill the earth with the knowledge of His glory, in His own way and time. Habakkuk would have to wait, as we often do (we will discuss that in the next chapter).

A Conversation

Prayer must be *both* speaking honestly from the heart *and* listening to the One to whom we speak. That is real conversation. When I began pastoring, there was a lady in our church who would call me, say what was on her mind and then, abruptly, just hang up. It was so frustrating! As I thought about it, though, I wondered if God felt the same way with most of my praying.

Jesus told His disciples, and us, that those who hear will hear more (see Mark 4:21–25). If we fail to listen, the conversation is over. Those biblical prayers that I alluded to, the prayers of Abraham, Moses and the prophets, included hearing. If we say, "Lord, help me," we need to listen to hear how He wants to help us.

God's voice, or answer, can come in various ways when we watch and listen. As in my own experience, the answer is not always immediate, but it comes when we are able to hear it. Hearing requires a receiver tuned to the proper frequency. There are millions of sounds in the air at any given moment, but we must have a radio, television, computer, cell phone or some other instrument in order to receive them. A pure heart tuned to God will hear.

1 Kings 19:12 records that the Lord spoke to Elijah in a "still small voice," not in the strong wind, earthquake or fire. He could not speak to Elijah while Elijah was running from Jezebel or hiding in the cave. Elijah had to come out of his cave and get into the place where he could receive the "signal." Too often our receiver "drops the call" because we are in the wrong place to receive it.

The Word as a Light

We are often in the dark about our conditions and our real needs. As we approach the Lord, we are coming to the Light and to Truth. "For with You is the fountain of life; in Your light we see light" (Psalm 36:9). According to John 1, Jesus Himself is life and light. The power and nature of light is fascinating; we can even use it for communication through fiber optics. Light travels at a speed of 186,000 miles per second—and it scatters darkness at the same speed.

When God speaks, things come to pass (Isaiah 42:9). As it is written in Genesis 1, "God said," and it was. He created all things through Jesus, the eternal Word (see Colossians 1:16; John 1:1–3). The words of God have a creative power in our lives, and they bring light that chases away the darkness. Why would we not listen?

Isaiah 50 is a powerful prophetic passage that described the trial of Jesus seven hundred years before it happened. Verse 4 tells us that Jesus was awakened morning by morning to hear and be encouraged, and by that He was able to encourage the weary. It all starts with hearing God's voice. Jesus was able to bear the shame, spitting and beatings because He heard. He did not walk in the light of His own sparks (see verses 10–11). Self-starting may sound good, but when we burn up all our own energy, hearing God renews us (see 2 Corinthians 3:17–4:1).

It is important to remember that God can use many means to speak to us. My focus here is to encourage us to get into His presence and hear, but He can address us in other ways, even unexpectedly. Reading the Bible is a good opportunity for the Lord to speak; after all, it is His Word. A pastor or some other leader may say something that we instantly know is for us. A friend may speak the Word to us, even in an offhanded way. If we are sensitive, we can say, "Yes, Lord."

The Energizing Word

Hearing God sustains and encourages us. I well remember one Sunday night when I was especially discouraged. Members of our church had gone away, finances were down, many were angry with me and I was reminding God that being a preacher was never my idea. Some of those who were attending only came to report to others what was or was not happening. We had Sunday evening services, and the time was drawing near for me to preach. I was on the floor in my office reminding the Lord of my situation. Finally, I got quiet. Then I heard, *What then shall we say to these things? If God is for us, who can be against us* (Romans 8:31)? The truth and power of that statement shot through me and stood me on my feet!

Almost immediately I was guided to Philippians 4, and the phrase "in the Lord" caught my attention (see Philippians 4:1–13). I was amazed at how often Paul used that phrase. I realized that I was not in trouble, I was in the Lord; I could rejoice. I remembered that even in jail, Paul had been "in the Lord." He was more aware of the Lord than the situation. When I entered the pulpit, I could hardly speak from wanting to laugh out loud. The joy of the Lord was my strength. Sure, the crowd was small and the situation had not changed. But I had—I was in the Lord. I delivered my message on what we can do when we realize that we are in the Lord and not just in the world, and I did laugh as I spoke.

On the way out the door, a lady, who seemed to be the head of the "telephone committee," said, "You should not be so happy at a time like this." I just smiled and almost laughed out loud. I was in the Lord; she, apparently, was not. I learned a lesson; when I am sad and miserable, the enemy is glad. When I am glad, he is miserable! I would rather see him miserable than me.

The Word of the Lord sustains us; it lifts us up out of the miry clay and sets our feet upon the Rock (see Psalm 40:1–3). It also changes our lives and situations. We live and move and have our being in Him (see Acts 17:22–28).

As I wrote earlier, the Lord visited me in our church in 1964. The resulting embracing of spiritual gifts was unusual in my denomination, and leaders felt the need to investigate. I was invited to sit with a committee of these leaders, tell my experience and defend it with Scripture. This I did as humbly and truthfully as I could.

After the meeting, a leading pastor took me aside, wanting to take up another matter: He asked me how we had racially integrated our church. This was Alabama in 1964; prior to that time, most churches in our area were segregated. He had wanted to integrate his church but was voted down by his congregation. This pastor had signed petitions to integrate local buses and had worked to improve race relations. I was not an activist, but nevertheless our church had become integrated. He was puzzled. "So tell me, Charles, how did you integrate your church?"

I waited on the Lord. "I did not integrate our church; the Holy Spirit did. The One who integrated our fellowship is the same One over whom you are investigating us." He walked away, no doubt still puzzled.

That Still, Small Voice

Later, that same pastor and I were called to debate the doctrine and work of the Holy Spirit before a large group of students. As far as I was concerned, I won that debate based on Scripture. I felt vindicated when a student, who led the closing prayer, prayed to be baptized in the Holy Spirit.

Later, that same pastor and I were called on to debate again before a large group of pastors. The other pastor led off with the same arguments based on "Corinthian immaturity and confusion." As I listened to him repeat the same themes as before, I thought, *This will be easy.* I had a large folder full of biblical notes. But then the Lord said something very unpleasant in that crucial moment.

You are not going to use your notes.

I resisted. "But, Lord, this can't be You!"

Listen to him, the Lord continued. *You have given him that impression—the "Corinthian impression." He sees you as immature, just emotional. I want you to apologize.*

"But, Lord, I cannot apologize for the Holy Spirit."

No, you cannot. Apologize for yourself and that you have not given a better impression of the Holy Spirit!

So, finally, my turn came, and though I did not relish it, I said, "Brothers, as I have listened to what our brother has to say, I realize that I have given the wrong impression of the Holy Spirit; I have been immature and even proud. I ask you to forgive me, and I'll try to do better in the future."

"Is that all?" the moderator asked.

"Yes, that is all." I sat down.

It was very quiet. After the gathering one minister came to me and said, "I don't know what happened to you, but whatever it was, it made a Christian out of you." Of course, the answer that I gave in the debate was not my own; it was from the Holy Spirit—that "still, small voice."

God does sometimes speak through signs, but that is usually to those who do not hear that still, small voice (see Matthew 12:39).

Revealed by the Spirit

John the Baptist recognized Jesus, though not by signs. At this point, Jesus had yet to show any signs. John recognized Jesus by the Spirit (see John 1:29–34). The apostle Paul said that he also knew men after the Spirit (see 2 Corinthians 5:16). He did not even know Jesus in the flesh, but only in the Spirit. Spiritual sensitivity, or listening to the Holy Spirit, is how we come to know Jesus and His will for our lives.

The Holy Spirit may also speak to us through friends—in fact, so can the enemy. It is vital to have true friends who tell us the truth. At one point I knew that the Lord wanted me to move to another location. I believed the Lord was leading me to a certain small town, but three close friends, John Duke, Glen Roachelle and Terry Parker, felt otherwise. I trusted them, so I listened to them and decided to visit the place that they thought the Lord had chosen. We had a meeting in that town, and a large crowd gathered. During the meeting, a man who had no knowledge of my plans prophesied that my ministry would be redirected. He gave some details that witnessed to my own spirit. As I later gathered for prayer with others, the Holy Spirit fell in power, and we all prostrated ourselves before the Lord. Needless to say, my friends were right.

I will say again, it is important to have the right friends.

Jesus told His generation over and over to be careful how they heard His voice. The people of His day failed to hear (though some did). Jesus had taught the ways of peace, but they listened instead to the voices of rebellion. Their failure to hear brought unimaginable calamity upon their nation. Roman atrocities were extreme to the point of stretching the imagination. The Jews resisted the Romans at the Antonia Fortress and at Masada, but they were brutally crushed, not rising again as a nation for almost two thousand years.

Our ways may seem right to us, but His ways lead to life, while ours lead to death (see Proverbs 14:12; Isaiah 53:6; 55:8–9).

What might we miss when we fail to hear? Ours is a communication and information society. Every school has courses on how to speak. There are, however, very few on how to listen. It took years for me to realize that I needed to listen, and much depends on listening. We do not learn when we speak, but we do when we listen.

If there ever was a time that we needed to hear, I believe it is now. What is the Lord saying to us now—through His Word, the Spirit, friends, parents, pastors and circumstances? May the Lord give us ears to hear! Sometimes we do have to wait before God speaks, and in the following chapter, we will talk about waiting on the Lord.

Discussion Questions

1. Name some ways that you have heard from God.

2. What has the Lord said to you in the past?

3. What is He saying to you now?

4. What outcomes in your life came as a result of hearing from God?

5. What outcomes can you point to from *not* hearing from God?

6. What is the Lord saying about your nation?

7. How much time do you devote to listening?

14

Do I Have to Wait?

"To everything there is a season, a time for every purpose under heaven . . ." (Ecclesiastes 3:1). Timing is everything. We can do the right thing at the wrong time and reduce the effect of our action. Being sensitive to the timing of God is a key to effectiveness in prayer.

We have a yellow Labrador at our house. He is an alpha male, muscular and full of energy. He loves to chase a ball or anything that we might throw, and he will bring it back. There are two problems, though. He does not understand the word *wait* and he only knows one speed—fast! This causes a few problems. A mature and well-trained dog, on the other hand, can understand and obey the command *Wait!*

So it is with us. As we mature, we learn to wait on the Lord. His time is not ours, and timing is everything. We can pray, as we should, but often the answer comes only as we wait.

At age 65, my father was nearing retirement. "Retire," of course, means you get tired more than once before you finally tire out. My parents had been at their church for 35 years, and they had a tiring time just prior to Dad's retirement. I wanted to do something special for him and my mother, but the Lord said, *Wait*. It was hard to wait because of my love for them and their need for encouragement. But the Lord had not said, *No*; He just said, *Wait*.

So I waited until after he retired. Then some friends and I did several things to show our love, including giving him a cruise, a car and a new opportunity to pastor senior adults in our church. The timing was just right, and he was reinvigorated. He worked with us for almost twenty more years.

God's time to act may be immediately, months in the future or after many years. When we have to wait, our faith will be tested. We may ask, "Did the Lord hear my prayer?" It would help to read and study the Bible for examples of waiting. One such example is found in Genesis 15:13–16: The Lord told Abraham that his descendants would be servants in a foreign land and be afflicted for four hundred years, after which they would come out and return to Canaan. He then told Abraham that the wickedness of the Amorites was not yet complete. It seems that God Himself was waiting on certain conditions to be ready. God does not abort the process.

In the biblical sense, waiting is not passive, though it does require a pause. Waiting is a delayed result for which we look with expectation and eagerness. So when we pray and sense that God has heard us, we expect the answer will come in God's time and are eager to see it.

The Lord spoke to Habakkuk in Habakkuk 2, saying that He would fill the earth with the knowledge of His glory, as the waters cover the sea. But He also said,

> For the vision is yet for an appointed time; but at the end it will speak, and it will not lie. Though it tarries, wait for it; because it will surely come, it will not tarry. Behold the proud, his soul is not upright in him; but the just shall live by his faith.
>
> Habakkuk 2:3–4

"The just shall live by his faith" is repeated in the New Testament and is the phrase that spoke to Martin Luther when he led the Reformation. It is, however, important to understand the context in Habakkuk. The vision was that the Lord would fill the earth with the knowledge of His glory. The proud could not wait, but it would happen.

Those That Wait

Great promises often require patient expectation to see them come to pass, even beyond our lifetime. That is real faith in words from God. One of my father's favorite models was George Mueller (1805–1898). Mueller was a German-born minister who built orphanages in England by an unusual faith in God's provision. In addition to loving orphans, Mueller loved and prayed for nonbelievers. In one case a man came to Christ 36 years after Mueller first began praying for him. By the time the man came to Christ, Mueller had already died.

When our daughter went to Costa Rica to work with orphans, she had no money, she did not know Spanish and she was single. She had Mueller's faith. She enrolled in a Spanish-language Bible school, graduated and began to work in a barrio occupied by the poor. She then met a woman who befriended her and taught her the culture. After that step she met her future husband, had foster children and purchased land. In the process, a donor we had not known previously gave her $100,000 toward the cost of the land. Through some tough years, they now have the land and a house, and they are building other houses. She had a vision but had to wait for it. Meanwhile she worked toward it with expectation of its fulfillment.

Psalm 27:14 is one of my favorites: "Wait on the LORD; be of good courage, and He shall strengthen your heart; wait, I say, on the LORD!" Twice David says, "Wait on the Lord," the second time with an exclamation point. David knew a lot about waiting and often spoke about it. He was anointed to be king of Israel while still a shepherd boy. It was many years and trials later that it actually came to pass. He had to first fight a giant and then endured Saul's anger and jealousy.

The apostle Paul, like the other apostles, understood the necessity of waiting and warring in expectation. He told Timothy to wage warfare according to the prophecies that had been made to Timothy. The Lord had spoken things to Timothy by prophetic gifts, and these prophecies required some battles while he waited in expectation for the fulfillment.

David, Paul, Timothy and each of us will have to wait for some promises to come to pass. Meanwhile we must not be passive but hold fast in patience and perseverance, struggling as necessary to get to the place of fulfillment. That was the case with Israel as the people journeyed to the Promised Land, believing with patience; perseverance amid contests is an ingredient for the inheritance. Many of them could not wait.

Jesus reminded His disciples of the patience that would be required of them, in that they would suffer great persecution. In that persecution He would tell them what to say. In Luke 21:19 He said, "By your patience possess your souls." They had a model of patience in Jesus (see Hebrews 6:15). God Himself is patient; He waits in expectation (see James 5:7).

Our culture does not promote patience; it promotes instant gratification with fast food, rapid transportation, instant communication and a host of delivery services, even for pizza. This is all fine, but God is not our "delivery man." The best results are not always the quickest.

I am impatient by nature, and my preference is "Five minutes ago!" I have had to learn that my clock and God's do not run the same way. It has not been easy, and sometimes my frustration and impatience have delayed the desired result. I once arrived at a city a week early for an appointment. In my impatience, I failed to properly read my calendar! I waited at the airport for the host to meet me and finally called him.

"Where are you?" he asked.

"I am at the airport."

"Airport? Brother Charles, you are a week early!"

That, needless to say, was embarrassing.

I am comforted by the disciples' example: "Lord, will You *at this time* restore the kingdom to Israel?" (Acts 1:6, emphasis mine). The Lord's answer was clear: "It is not for you to know times or seasons which the Father has put in His own authority" (verse 7). They wanted it, and they wanted it then and there. Unfortunately for them, they were a few centuries too early. His answer was a rebuke of impatience. They did, however, learn patience, they possessed their souls and they persevered through persecution. They learned to watch and pray. So can we.

Not *Why* but How

One of the great mysteries of the Bible, and life itself, is why the eternal God, who has all power, wants us to pray and work with Him in carrying out His eternal will. I cannot answer that question, but He does want our participation in His plan. What a privilege to co-labor with God. My purpose is not to answer *why* we have to wait but to learn *how* to wait. That is the way He wants it, and He is our God.

There are many questions that I cannot answer: Why suffering? Why evil? Why does God allow some to be martyred? Or, why I was born for this place and time? The issue is not why but how I can accomplish His will and purpose in my life. If we get lost in the *why*, we will never get the *how*, and then we will be paralyzed.

Ideas do have consequences, both good and bad. Philosophers major in ideas and often fail to see the consequences—such was the case with Marx and Nietzsche, whose ideas brought terrible consequence to the world. In the case of a Christian, God has the idea and we do the obeying. That brings good results, though we often must wait. Isaiah 64:4 tells us that God acts for the one who waits for Him. Another favorite passage is Isaiah 40:28–31, which says that those who wait on the Lord will renew their strength.

While waiting sometimes takes a long time, this is not always the case. I recently met with a man who was in financial need, though he did not tell me—I believe that the Lord showed me. As our visit concluded, we prayed and then I was impressed to give him $100. He had not asked for it and even offered a mild protest. But I insisted, telling him that it was only a seed that I wanted to plant in his life. That very evening I met with another couple for prayer, and at the conclusion of our prayer time, during which we waited on the Lord, they gave me a check for $10,000 for the ministry! I had not mentioned finances. Seeds do not usually sprout so fast, but that one did. I was astounded!

I suppose that because waiting has been such a struggle for me, I have great awe for those who have waited for the Lord, even beyond their own lifetimes. They are described this way:

> . . . of whom the world was not worthy. They wandered in deserts and mountains, in dens and caves of the earth. And all these, having obtained a good testimony through faith, did not receive the promise, God having provided something better for us, that they should not be made perfect apart from us.
>
> Hebrews 11:38–40

They waited and we reaped. They believed the promises and paid the price, and we have received. That is often the case.

Praying Large Prayers

Waiting can be brief or prolonged, depending on the nature of our prayers. Jesus taught us to pray for daily bread. That is not a long wait. But He also said to pray, "Thy Kingdom come, Thy will be done on earth as it is in heaven." The manifestation of the Kingdom of God was a different matter; that required centuries. In the same prayer Jesus mentioned two different degrees of waiting, both of which required faith. Apparently, praying for the Kingdom to come requires a greater faith and perseverance.

We should pray about our own immediate needs, but we should also pray large prayers, prayers beyond our own needs, such as for future generations, the nation, the economy, the suffering Church around the world and God's Kingdom to come on earth. As we cooperate with God, can we hear His concerns? Hearing from God brings us to the big picture. The larger the prayer, the more waiting is required.

I ask myself this question: Am I a worthy heir of those who gave their very lives that I could be the completion of their faith? Is it enough that I reap the rewards, or should I be willing to sow my life so that others can be the completion of *my* faith? Can I pray large prayers that may require waiting beyond my lifetime? Can I be both patient and expectant for the return of the Lord (see James 5:7–8; 2 Peter 3:1–9)? Can I, like George Mueller, pray for the nonbeliever who may not meet the Lord until I pass on into the presence of God?

I grew up with the view that the end of the age was very near. There was always speculation about the return of Christ and who the Antichrist might be. When the Jesus Movement exploded in the 1960s, some would not go to college because they thought Jesus would return before they would need a college education. The immediacy of my and others' mentalities precluded the notion of waiting and preparation. Some forgot that "times and seasons" are in God's hands; the large view of history was not understood. Our focus must be on obedience, preparation and a willingness to wait, not on dates and times. Dates have routinely been set, and they have always been wrong! Prayer is about cooperating with God in His business on earth, not about speculation. Even as I write this, some believe the end will come before I finish this book.

Vigilance is always a virtue; speculation is not. Speculation is the result of pride and impatience. It may satisfy curiosity but not reality. Expectation is a virtue, but speculation is a vice.

In the mid-1960s, I believed that the Lord promised a great revival in China, and I gave a prophetic word to that effect. At that time it seemed far off, but now I think there are more born-again believers in China than any other country in the world. It took some waiting and a lot of persecution, even some martyrdom, but it came to pass. I thank God for those to whom the promise meant more than their very lives. Such continues to be the case in the Middle East, Sudan, Nigeria and other places. These Christians not only wait, but they persevere and are worthy heirs of the saints of Hebrews 11.

Habakkuk declares,

> Though the fig tree may not blossom, nor fruit be on the vines; though the labor of the olive may fail, and the fields yield no food; though the flock may be cut off from the fold, and there be no herd in the stalls—yet I will rejoice in the LORD, I will joy in the God of my salvation.
>
> Habakkuk 3:17–18

Habakkuk was a true prophet and man of God. His faith was not in immediate results but in God. We can contrast that with those whose cry for immediacy drives them from place to place in search of instant gratification; that will not bring great results.

But those who believe and endure will see great rewards. Do not underestimate the power of waiting, perseverance and faith. God values it highly! That is what got us here—our forefathers and mothers who endured, believing for something better for us. That kind of faith will sustain those who come after us. I pray that those who follow us will call us blessed as we blessed the heroes of the past.

If we are to endure and reap the great rewards of waiting on God, we must learn what it means to "pray without ceasing," and we will discuss that next.

―――――― Discussion Questions ――――――

1. What does it mean to wait on the Lord?

2. What does waiting require of us?

3. What should we do while we wait?

4. Do you have a vision worth waiting for?

5. Name some biblical examples of those who waited.

6. Do you have people on your prayer list who you are waiting to see meet the Lord?

7. What are other "large prayers" in your prayer life?

8. What are some things God is waiting for?

15

Is He Always on My Mind?

The Grammy-winning song "Always on My Mind," made famous in versions by Brenda Lee, Elvis Presley and Willie Nelson, tells the story of a man who in retrospect realized that he had not adequately expressed his love and gratitude to the one whom he loved. It is a beautiful, if somewhat sad, song, and it is difficult for me to listen to given that my dear wife passed away in 2008. Looking back, we all could wish that our expressions of love had been more adequate than they were.

As I contemplate praying without ceasing, which Paul instructs in 1 Thessalonians 5:17, I recall that beautiful song and how it relates to our relationship with God. Is He always on our minds?

I grew up in church; that was where we "met God." Later I realized that God does not want us simply to visit Him at church; He wants to walk with us through life. It is good to meet the Lord at church but sad not to realize that He desires to go with us when we leave. He wants to be always on our minds, as we are on His.

When we contemplate prayer, we often think of special times when we turn aside from life and enter the realm of the Spirit, and those can and should be special. But living our daily lives, we can have numerous special times if we are aware that the Lord is with us continually. Spiritual maturity requires that we transition from "sometimes" to "all times."

We cannot be in church all the time; in fact, our commission is to go into the world to be the light of the world. We can only accomplish this if He is always on our minds while we are in the world. Awareness is the key to praying without ceasing.

Many years ago, a book called *The Practice of the Presence of God* affected many people, including me. Its author, Brother Lawrence (1611–1691), was a Carmelite lay brother in Paris. He served as a cook for the monastic order, which focused on contemplative prayer. The key to his teachings is that he learned to see the Lord's presence in his work. Even in the most mundane tasks, he saw God's presence, writing that "the time of business does not with me differ from the time of prayer."

The apostle Paul said it this way: "To be spiritually minded is life and peace" (Romans 8:6). To be spiritually minded is to have a mind set on the Spirit, even as one walks in daily life. On the other hand, a mind continually set on our physical desires brings death, for we consume ourselves. The lesson here is that the mind is the eye of life: Wherever we focus our minds will determine the outcome.

A Practical Truth

That truth has many practical results. Recently I was headed west on Interstate 10. I like to drive, though sometimes my attention has drifted away from driving and to my cell phone, which has resulted in tickets but fortunately not death. Sometimes I have gotten absorbed in the news or some other matter and missed a turn. Thankfully, I have a GPS. On this particular trip, however, I received a warning from the Lord: *Slow down.* I obeyed.

Just ahead of me was a large truck hauling a load of steel. As I slowed down, the tires on that truck began to peel off, and the truck swerved across the lanes of the highway. Steel-belted rubber was spraying everywhere, but by slowing down I was able to avoid the truck and the flying rubber. Gratitude filled my heart as I realized what the Lord had just saved me from. I was inspired to pray without ceasing the rest of the trip. The Lord knows what is up ahead.

Watch and Pray

In Matthew 26:41, Jesus told His disciples to "watch and pray, lest you enter into temptation. The spirit indeed is willing, but the flesh is weak." He knew the Tempter was ahead. The disciples had fallen asleep while Jesus was praying about His imminent crucifixion—the most important event in history. After His warning, they went back to sleep. In a matter of hours Peter would deny three times that he even knew Jesus. He and the others would scatter in fear, leaving Jesus to die with only John and Mary standing with Him.

He had warned them to stay alert, but they slept instead. History reveals that we often run the "red lights" that the Lord has placed in our paths only to collide with onrushing reality.

Texting while driving is now illegal in many places, and for good reason. Many young people, and others, have been killed due to texting while driving—a minor matter took their minds off the major issue. So it is in our lives when our minds become focused on some issue of lesser importance than God's perspective. Whatever is on our minds will determine our focus—or loss of focus—and can lead to death.

If the Lord's own disciples could miss the moment, so can we. "Watch and pray" is good advice for all of us. We cannot afford to miss the reality before us even at this moment of history. There is a truck directly ahead, in our path, and its wheels are coming off. Be afraid? No. Be aware, and be prepared. The truck is probably not driving through the church, but it is on the road that you will drive in life. Practice the Presence.

The key to praying all the time is not speaking to God all the time; rather it is the awareness of His presence and continually listening to Him. Jesus said, "I am with you always" (see Matthew 28:20). If we believe that, then we have the privilege of continual communication. As I said, my current car has a GPS; the voice is not *always* speaking, but it is always there. I would do well to always listen for it.

Praying always, in and with the Holy Spirit's guidance, is not mystical or "otherworldly"; it is for this world, to give us practical guidance in everyday life. We do not need to always be talking, only always listening. He is our divine "GPS."

Unceasing Prayer

The apostle Paul told the Colossians that he did not cease to pray for them (see Colossians 1:9). They were always on his mind. He said much the same to the Thessalonians (see 2 Thessalonians 1:11). Apparently, Paul continually prayed for the churches. I wonder if the health of our churches is always on our minds. Paul reminded the Roman Christians to be continually steadfast in prayer as they served one another in the church (see Romans 12:9–12). I also wonder what would happen in our churches if we continued steadfast in our prayers for their condition.

I believe in planning and strategy, which I view as part of being a responsible person. When I leave for a trip, I preprogram my GPS to a certain destination. But life is not preprogrammed, though the Lord does have a destiny for us; it is often what we do not expect that alters our plan. A speeding ticket or an accident is not part of our plan. Life is full of the unexpected, but we can be prepared if we listen.

The communist leadership in the U.S.S.R. had plans—five-year plans, ten-year plans and more. They preprogrammed their plans but ignored the God factor. Their plans did not include their demise. I have heard many plans proposed by church, political and business leaders—beautiful plans—but often unplanned things occurred on their way to Utopia. They had a plan but apparently missed some guidance. It is good to plan, but it is also good to listen as we drive toward their fulfillment. *Continual* or *unceasing* do not mean sporadic or spasmodic.

The Bible does not give many verses about Enoch, but it does say that he consistently lived and walked with God for 300 years. One day they could not find Enoch because "God took him" (see Genesis 5:24; Hebrews 11:5). The book of Hebrews tells us that he was translated by faith (he is one of the heroes listed in Hebrews 11). Enoch had a 365-year relationship with God and "walked" with God. That certainly occurred in his daily life, out in the fields, woods and villages. That is where we need to walk with God. His fellowship with Enoch did not depend on church facilities.

In addition we should note that Enoch escaped the flood by walking with God and being translated into the very presence of God that he enjoyed during his life on earth. What makes us think that we would enjoy heaven if we do not enjoy the presence of God here on earth? I am amazed that before Noah, Abraham, Moses, the prophets and even Jesus and the apostles, Enoch knew and loved God's presence, and his story lived through the flood and subsequent centuries. Noah knew it, and he, too, heard from God. Noah's contemporaries apparently did not. But Enoch's story survived, and it should inspire us to walk with God in our world.

145

Nature does not leave a vacuum; something else moves in when a vacuum appears. If we allow a vacuum of God in our lives, our families or other areas, it will be filled with something else. If the Lord is not leading us, something else will. If the Lord is not leading our nation, something else will. The vacuum that has existed is the direct result of our leaving the Holy Spirit at church—if even there. If we walk with the Lord in continuous fellowship, there will never be a vacuum in our lives.

Perhaps someone should write a hymn to Jesus that says, "You are always on my mind." No wonder Jesus said that men always ought to pray and not lose heart (see Luke 18:1).

Are we willing to hear Him unconditionally? Are we ready to obey when He speaks? Let's examine that next.

Discussion Questions

1. How can we pray without ceasing?

2. Why should we?

3. Give two examples of people who did.

4. What if we do not?

5. What might happen in our lives if we develop a continual awareness of the Holy Spirit?

6. Can you recall decisions that you regret and why you made them?

7. What impact on the church might there be if we practice the presence of God in daily life?

16

Do I Give Him a Blank Check?

My Iranian friend had a pastor who was martyred for His service to Jesus. He wrote a check to God, signed it and gave his life unconditionally. In this chapter, let us look at what it means to give God a blank check and how He might fill it in.

In many ways the Lord has given to each of us a signed check with the amount not specified—a blank check that we fill in. I say that based on the statements He made to His disciples in John 14–16 (see John 14:13; 15:16; 16:23–24). In each statement He said, "Whatever you ask in My name . . ." That is amazing: He gives us His name and says, "Ask whatever."

Throughout this book we have discussed conditions in prayer, such as faith, forgiveness, righteousness and perseverance. There are conditions to prayer, including our desire for His will above ours. And yet He still says to ask for whatever we desire in His name—nothing is off the table.

The Father esteems the name of Jesus, His unique and eternal Son. When we approach Him in the name of Jesus, it shows Him that we understand the mission of Christ to bring us into fellowship with Him through forgiveness of our sin. When Jesus' name is "on the check," the Father sees His authority, His cleansing and His riches (see Philippians 4:19). No one else has the authority to write a check on the Father's account. Jesus alone has power of attorney. If the Father chooses to answer someone's prayer who fails to mention Jesus, that is certainly within His sovereign prerogative, but my task as a believer is to pray the way He taught us.

If my prayer is to be effective, I must regard His name in life as well as in prayer. The Father takes it seriously when we misuse or misrepresent the Lord's name. That is for our protection, so that when we pray, we are attributing the highest value to the Name that gives us access.

Covenant

Jesus made a covenant with us in His blood, a bond that made us one with Him. When we receive communion, we are remembering that covenant and are warned to do so in reverence to His body and blood (see Luke 22:14–20; 1 Corinthians 11:17–34). Again, we are receiving the person most holy to us and the sacrifice He made for us. Casual attitudes toward Him and His name produce casualties. If our prayers are important as we fill in the blank—our petition—then the name at the bottom is all-important.

The name of Jesus was vital to the apostles—sacred. He made the New Covenant with them. They preached in His name, they prayed in His name, they healed in His name and they suffered for His name. Because they all revered His name so highly, the Father regarded them highly and answered their prayers.

Our culture lacks regard for the name of Jesus. Christians often unwittingly fail to reverence the name of Jesus by using Jesus' name as a religious habit. I heard of one person who said, "The devil is after me; bless His holy name." When I was pastoring my first church, one member said "Amen!" often, but only out of habit. Once I was preaching so rapidly that when I cleared my throat, he said "Amen!" His *amen* meant nothing. (I do appreciate an *amen* when it registers from the heart.)

If we do not use Jesus' name as a habit but in true reverence, it will have a positive effect on us, others and most of all the Father (see Malachi 3:16). The holy reverence of His name is the beginning of wisdom (see Psalm 111:10). Because I reverence His name, when I close my prayer, I say, "In the name of Jesus." It is not a magic formula but an acknowledgment of who He is and what He has done to make my prayer a reality.

Obedience

Now that we have discussed this holy name that has authorized our right to access the Father, let us discuss our obedience in response to what He might say. He has signed a blank check— "Whatever you ask in my name." Do we now give Him a blank check? Do we sign our will and resources over to Him and His will? The same name on the check He has given us is on the "work order" that He will give us. How we revere His name in prayer is revealed by how we respond to His guidance.

Have you ever had someone come to you for advice and you sensed before you gave it that they would not heed it? How did that affect you? If we come to God having "filled in the blank" with limitations on how much He can draw on us, does it really work? We received from God a blank check, a "whatever" check, and we returned to God a signed check, but for only $5.28 worth of obedience. How does that work with God?

The great heroes of history and today have given God a signed check and allowed Him to fill in the blank. Often the Lord filled in the blank with "everything you have" or "your life" (see Matthew 16:24–27). Too many Christians in our time are writing very small checks. What I mean is this kind of prayer: *Lord, if You do this, then I'll do this.* That is a small check. A bigger check would be *If You do this, then I'll do whatever You say.*

Jeremiah was given a very difficult message that would bring him severe persecution (see Jeremiah 1:1–19; 9:1–11). At times he wished that he had never been born (see Jeremiah 15:10; 20:14). His prophetic mission was to declare God's Word whatever the cost, and his obedience brought him trouble.

When the Lord called me to preach, I had a vague idea that it might cause others and myself trouble. I have said that if I ever wrote an autobiography, I would title it *I Didn't Mean to Cause Trouble.* More than once I reminded the Lord that preaching was not my idea and stated my reservations and limitations before I answered, but finally I signed the check. My devotion and sacrifice have often been flawed and are in no measure comparable to that of others. But I signed it. You can be assured that when you sign the check, He will fill in the blank.

More to Come?

I have wondered more than once: What if God is still filling in the blank? What if He is still requiring more of me than I had imagined? I think of those in our time who are giving their very lives for His name's sake; would I be able to write that check?

A lot of us have written checks that bounced because of "insufficient funds." *I'll do whatever,* we say. *I love You, but I can't tithe, witness to others or lose my reputation for talking about Jesus* (see Mark 8:38).

Our nation should have known much earlier, but on September 11, 2001, we learned that we have enemies who are willing to die destroying us and all that we stand for. They are serious. Those who are not serious have little hope in overcoming those who are. I find radical Islam detestable, but what concerns me even more is the tepid response of Christians to the cause of Christ.

The apostles whom we revere and quote were intense and even radical in fulfilling their mission, and they were successful. But form will not prevail against fire.

My appeal in this chapter is twofold: Revere the name through which we pray, and write the kind of commitment to Him that He gave to us, a large covenant check! What are the rewards of doing those two things? The possibilities are numerous. We can glorify His great name in the earth and receive power in our prayers. We can once again discover His purpose in the earth and in our lives. We can give our children, a generation currently leaving the Church, a worthy legacy of true faith. And we can see people come to Jesus. That will bring joy in heaven.

There are times when rewards are delayed and prayer does not seem to work. How do we handle that? We will examine that question next.

Discussion Questions

1. How has Jesus given us a blank check that He signed?

2. How important is His name? Why?

3. What does His name, Jesus, mean?

4. In what way can we give God a blank check?

5. Name some people of the Bible who gave God a blank check.

6. What might result if we gave God whatever He might desire?

7. Do you believe that the Lord is still filling in the check that you wrote when you first trusted Him? What may He be asking of you?

17

What Do I Do When It Does Not Seem to Be Working?

"Why wasn't my prayer answered?" is a question that all of us have asked at some point in our lives. We have prayed and received no perceptible response. Some people handle that better than others because they trust the Lord anyway. Others stumble if they believe that God was not listening. Still others go on praying routinely and never question why nothing is happening.

In the previous chapter we discussed Jesus' statement that we could ask whatever we desire in His name. That is not all He said about prayer, however. In John 15:7, He said, "If you abide in Me, and My words abide in you, you will ask what you desire, and it shall be done for you." There are conditions to asking whatever we desire and receiving what we asked. He went on to speak of abiding in His love and keeping His commandments. We have also discussed elements that are involved in effective praying: reverence for God, faith, forgiveness, the Holy Spirit, passion, endurance and obedience.

I am not one who believes that God hears all prayers; in fact, I have alluded to Scriptures that clearly indicate He does not (see Isaiah 59:1–2; Matthew 6:5–8; Luke 18:9–17). If our hearts and motives are not right, we have a problem (see James 4:1–3).

There is truth to the Garth Brooks song "Unanswered Prayers": Sometimes God keeps silent because it would not be good for us if He gave us what we wanted. It is not unusual to get something through hard work only to discover that it does not satisfy us as we thought it would. The Lord knows.

Sometimes He does hear but says, *Not yet*. Other things must happen before He will answer the prayer. And then there are times when people pray in opposition—"Lord, give us rain!" at the same time as "Lord, keep it dry!"

A more serious example of praying in opposition occurs during war. During the world wars there were Christians on both sides, and I am sure many were praying. There were also Christians on both sides during the American Civil War. General Robert E. Lee, commander of the Southern armies, was a devoted Christian and a man of prayer, but the South lost. Abraham Lincoln was also a Christian, and I have heard that, when asked if God was on their side, he answered, "My concern is not whether God is on our side. My great concern is whether we are on His side."

Hindrances

We have already discussed some hindrances to prayer, but I will reiterate them and list some more:

> *We are in sin*. If we are aware of sin in our lives, we must repent, which means to turn away. The Lord is unlikely to hear the prayer of someone who refuses to change.

We are praying from the mouth but not the heart (see Isaiah 29:13; Matthew 15:8). Empty words produce empty results. Mere form is devoid of power (see 2 Timothy 3:5).

A deacon in the first church that I pastored prayed the same prayer so often that I could repeat it: "Lord, as our pastor stands behind the sacred desk, hide him behind the cross." One day he got it reversed: "As our pastor stands behind the cross, hide him behind the sacred desk." I do not think that he or anyone noticed, including the Lord. It was a good prayer, but it was not from the heart.

It is not God's purpose. I am not a proponent of always adding the caveat "If it be Thy will." We have this assurance in 1 John 5:14–15: "Now this is the confidence that we have in Him, that if we ask anything according to His will, He hears us. And if we know that He hears us, whatever we ask, we know that we have the petitions that we have asked of Him." I believe that as we study His Word and fellowship with Him, we can know *before* we ask that we are praying according to His will. Scripture tells us what His will is.

We lack patience. We may conclude too soon that He did not hear us. Perhaps we need to persist and endure (see Psalm 27:13–14; Luke 18:1–8). When Jesus said, "Ask, seek and knock," He meant continually asking, seeking, and knocking. Saul lost his kingdom, in part, because he was impatient (see 1 Samuel 13:1–14).

Something else needs to happen before God answers. In Scripture we sometimes find God waiting for something before answering prayers. He told Abraham that after serving four hundred years in a strange land, his descendants could return to Canaan; but before this could happen, the wickedness of the Amorites must be fully revealed (see Genesis 15:16). Joseph was given dreams that showed he would be a ruler, but he went through a long and difficult process before it came to pass (see Genesis 37–47). The

Lord gave Habakkuk a vision that the knowledge of His glory would cover the earth as the waters cover the seas, but that would take centuries.

We will not forgive. As we are praying, the Lord may call attention to someone we need to forgive. If we fail to do that, it will hinder our prayers (see Matthew 6:12–15).

Our prayers may be too self-centered (see James 4:1–3; Isaiah 58). The Lord is concerned for the whole world (see John 3:16). I believe that He gets weary of hearing, "Bless me," if we fail to bless others. The Lord is big hearted, and he wants to enlarge our hearts also.

We have ingratitude. We all have difficulty listening to those we know to be ungrateful, and ingratitude is the beginning of a downward spiral (see Romans 1:21). The Lord is speaking, but we are so locked into what we want that we cannot hear what He wants (see Isaiah 55:8–13). The Lord may be attempting to redirect us to a better place than the one we are seeking.

We may not be prepared to receive what we are asking for (see Luke 16:10–12). David was anointed to be king while he was yet a shepherd; he still had to kill a giant and mature. To get the prize we must endure the process. Great coaches do not begin training by focusing on the championship; they focus on the things that make champions.

We lack faith. Jesus said, "When you pray, believe" (see Mark 11:24; Hebrews 11:6). One man said, "I have had a lot of luck with my prayers lately." Prayer is not a matter of luck. Faith is a substantive confidence in God that He will hear and answer.

Fasting might help us focus on hearing God and increase our faith. Fasting is a denial of nourishment and pleasure in order to focus on a more serious issue (see Matthew 17:21). We have biblical examples of this in Jesus and Moses, who fasted 40 days, and Daniel, who fasted 21. We will discuss fasting further in chapter 19.

Do not be too quick to evaluate the effect of a prayer. Large prayers usually require more time. Sometimes answers come after we have forgotten that we even asked.

God and His Reasons

In 2 Corinthians 12:7–10, Paul speaks of his thorn in the flesh. He had asked the Lord to remove this "messenger of Satan," which was given to him so that he would not be exalted above measure in his numerous revelations. He asked that it be removed three times, but it, whatever it was, remained. The Lord's answer to this was, "My grace is sufficient for you, for My strength is made perfect in weakness" (verse 9). That was not what Paul asked for, but he received it anyway:

> Therefore most gladly I will rather boast in my infirmities, that the power of Christ may rest upon me. Therefore I take pleasure in infirmities, in reproaches, in needs, in persecutions, in distresses, for Christ's sake. For when I am weak, then I am strong.
>
> 2 Corinthians 12:9–10

Did Paul lack faith? I do not think so. In other places his faith is powerfully evident. He literally gave his life for Christ and the Gospel. He "poured himself out" as an offering to God (see 2 Timothy 4:6). Next to our Lord, there is no one I admire more. Did God answer him? Yes. God just gave a different answer than the one he requested. Paul's faith was not in an outcome, it was in God.

I find it remarkable that the Lord would inspire Paul to tell us this story, because we could otherwise assume that Paul always got what he asked. He did not, apparently, nor do we.

But that did not prevent him from continuing to pray—without ceasing. And it should not prevent us. I do not suggest that Paul was sick, and I would not use Paul's model as an explanation for a lack of healing. It simply says to me that some things have to be endured, and God will give us the grace to do so. In the process the Lord will mature us and reveal His glory (see Hebrews 5:7–9).

If our "faith" gets derailed because of an unfulfilled request, or one that is delayed, then our faith was in an outcome, not in the Lord.

Drew Dyck wrote a very good book, *Generation Ex-Christian*,[1] which describes the loss of our youth and how to approach those who have left the Lord and the Church. In the book he gives the testimony of Andrew Palau, son of Luis Palau, one of the most effective evangelists of this era. Andrew became a "classic prodigal," going away from God and out into the world. The Palaus prayed for their son many years with sensitivity to the Holy Spirit and to their son. Finally he returned and is serving the Lord. Like the original prodigal's father, the Palaus continued with diligence, compassion and vigilance. We reap in due season if we do not faint.

Only God can change hearts; we need to pray in faith and love as He does. Again, we must resist the temptation to evaluate our prayers during the process. As a boy I used to root azaleas and camellias. I would have to wait four to six weeks with the plants in the rooting box. I watered the cuttings every day and kept them from direct sunlight. I rooted thousands of cuttings that grew to be beautiful plants, but often I could not wait to see if they were growing roots. In a couple of weeks, I would pull a cutting to check it out. If it was rooting, of course, I aborted the process.

1. Drew Dyck, *Generation Ex-Christian: Why Young Adults Are Leaving the Faith and How to Bring Them Back* (Chicago: Moody, 2010), 131–133.

Our prayer lives can be like that; we interrupt the process and impede the purpose. As I said in an earlier chapter, we must learn to wait on God. Most flowers do not mature in a day or even a week. God's work requires time.

"The Lord is not slack concerning His promise, as some count slackness, but is longsuffering toward us, not willing that any should perish but that all should come to repentance" (2 Peter 3:9). Peter understood quite well the Lord's patience from his own personal experience. We also must have patience if we are to be fruitful. Jesus prayed for all of us who would come after His life on the earth and would believe on His name (see John 17:20), and He is still praying for us (see Hebrews 7:25). That is the heart of Jesus in prayer: long term, steadfast and persistent. When one comes to Him, He rejoices but keeps on praying for others. Will everyone come to Him? No, but He has not stopped praying; nor should we, for some will come to Him. He never turns to the Father and says, "It isn't working."

It is good to review the reasons prayer may not be effective in order to be sure that we have not hindered our own prayers. But we also need to build our faith and joy by remembering prayers that *were* answered.

Keep the Story

I love a good story; it is a tradition in my family on the Scot-Irish side. God gave us a collection of His stories in the Bible. We remember the stories, and children love them. Scripture is filled with testimonies of God's grace and power. Our own testimony, when we have witnessed the Truth, is also our most powerful tool for advancing the Kingdom of God.

When you pray and receive an answer, write the story. I have a notebook filled with such answers to prayer. I could have had many more, but I did not write them down. The best stories are good testimonies of God's intervention in someone's life, for a *testi*mony tells of overcoming a test. It is good for us to occasionally review those stories to be reminded that prayer is effective, and so they can encourage others.

Once, after I had preached what I thought was a good message, a fellow minister came up to me and said, "Charles, you are a good preacher, but I love your story." I was actually taken aback because I thought he was minimizing the Word. In truth we need to know and declare the Word, but when we tell a story associated with the Word, it builds faith and makes the Word memorable. Write your story and tell it. People may argue with your theology, but they probably will not argue with your story.

The rewards of continuing in prayer, even when it seems futile, will create new stories, and the longer and harder you prayed, the greater the story! My dear friends Bishop Levy and Lady Delia Knox, whom I mentioned earlier, have one such story. Lady Delia was wheelchair bound for 22 years with a severed spinal column due to an accident, but then she was healed! She now walks and ministers. What a great story! Many people neither believe in miracles nor healing—but then, there is this story.

When we read or hear stories like that, it makes the stories in the Bible more real to us. Many reject the Bible because they have not heard a recent comparable story. We should pray for a great story in our own lives and in others' lives, and then tell them! Tell them often!

When you tell your story, you build both your faith and the faith of others. Jesus used stories to build faith and to correct false faith. And of course history is "His story." The Gospel is the greatest story ever told—the story of Jesus has changed hundreds of millions of lives.

A Story of Redemption

One of the men I pastor was himself a pastor until he developed an alcohol problem that cost him his family and his church. I remained his pastor, and he was like a prodigal son. A lot of people gave up on him, but I could not. He went through at least three rehab treatments. One rehab clinic was a famous treatment center, but he left early. Because he was a minister, there was little that people could tell him that was new.

Sometimes we would sit and talk while he was under the influence. This went on for about five years. Finally he came to the end of his journey in a "far country." When he came to himself, he began to help others by telling his story. In the ensuing years he has touched thousands of lives and taught hundreds of seminars. He is a good speaker, but he has an even greater story.

It can be disappointing when prayer does not seem to work, but give the Lord time and do not neglect your own story. What He has done for you, He can do for others. In case you do not believe that you have a story, I will reverse that: What He has done for others, He will do for you.

There is an answer if we persevere. In the next chapter I will give an example of a woman who did persevere for several years—even when by all appearances it did not seem to be working—and how she handled what she believed the Lord told her.

--- Discussion Questions ---

1. Name three hindrances to prayer.

2. Does God always answer prayer?

3. What are three important elements of effective praying?

4. Why should you give God time before analyzing your prayer?

5. Do you have a story about an answered prayer?

6. What did you learn from Paul's thorn in the flesh?

7. What does it mean if we become discouraged because an answer is delayed?

18

I Believe I Have Heard the Lord—What Should I Do Now?

A woman of strong character and convictions began coming to our church even though her husband was a deacon in another church. She came seeking the power of the Holy Spirit, which she felt was lacking in the other church. As a pastor I would have normally advised her to stay in her church with her husband. But as I listened to her, I decided to give it some time.

Their marriage was difficult as he, too, was a strong person and ran a large, successful business. She believed she had heard from the Lord to move to our church, and I did not want to contradict the guidance she had received, especially since she was a serious Bible student and had taught Sunday school. Not only did she obey what she had heard about coming to our church, she also believed that the Lord had given her guidance in how to reach her husband, who was manifesting behavior that was less than Christian. He was drinking heavily, though his church was opposed to drinking at all. She wanted to demonstrate the authenticity of her decision by the way she obeyed the Lord and treated her husband (see 1 Peter 3:1–6). Given that she had already violated his wishes about leaving his church, that would be a tough road.

This woman came to me for prayer many times as she struggled in her marriage, but she stood steadfast on the promise the Lord had given her. I talked with her father, himself an elderly Christian, who wept as he shared her struggles. It would be ten years before her husband got right with God. He suffered a heart attack and a stroke, and he was unconscious for days. Finally the Lord raised him up—as a new man. I will never forget the day he entered our church in new, childlike faith. His wife had indeed heard from God. My father, who was then the pastor of senior adults, became his pastor and remarked to me how childlike the man's prayers were.

Testing Our Guidance

The Lord speaks to us so that we will act on what we hear. But we should consider several issues before we do:

- Does what I think I heard agree with Scripture?
- Who will be affected by my action?
- Am I willing to deal with the consequences of my action?
- Have I sought counsel from other mature Christians?
- Am I willing to accept the possibility that I was mistaken or that I need to wait?

We often see people who think they have heard the Lord and do things in His name that He did not actually authorize. Some quote Acts 5:29 as justification for doing what they think they have heard: "We ought to obey God rather than men." Indeed, we should. But the apostles had a mature knowledge of the voice of the Lord, and they acted together. Even the apostle Paul submitted his revelations to the other apostles and elders (see Acts 15). We are not "lone rangers" acting independently; we are members of a local body, or should be.

Both Old Testament Law and Jesus required witnesses to establish truth (see Deuteronomy 17:6; 19:18; Matthew 18:16; 2 Corinthians 13:1). Paul required confirmation of vocal gifts brought to the Church (see 1 Corinthians 14:26–33). Having confirmation or an *amen* means that we are not alone in what we have heard and do not stand alone as we act on it (see Ecclesiastes 4:9–12).

To whom should we go for confirmation? First, we should examine the guidance in light of Scripture. (That is one reason to know the Bible.) Then we should go to a mature leader or our pastor. We can also go to praying friends who know us and will stand with us. A young person should go to their parents if they are believers, and in some cases even if they are not. A married person should consult his or her spouse—whoever is affected. In the case of the woman who left her husband's church, she did share what she heard with her spouse, but the guidance was rejected for obvious reasons. Nevertheless that woman did seek confirmation from me, and what she heard proved to be true.

An unwillingness to submit one's revelations is not a good sign, and I have witnessed sad results from unilateral action in opposition to advice. I know of thousands of dollars lost, divorce, division and other bad outcomes. When one acts unilaterally, that person must accept the consequence, but unfortunately others are affected as well.

Early on in my spiritual life, my father cautioned me about the spiritual realm in a way that humbled me and even put a holy fear in me. He was right. Some read astrology charts for guidance—a big mistake! The wrong friends can be a big mistake also, because they will give wrong guidance. We must be careful to whom we give the "steering wheel" of our lives. We all need leaders and peers who hear from God and whose lives are open to examination. Scripture says, "Recognize those who labor among you . . ." (1 Thessalonians 5:12). If we do not trust our leaders, we are in the wrong place. And if our guidance is different from theirs, we could end up sowing discord (see Proverbs 6:19).

Listening to the Right Voices

Growing up in a small community in the 1940s and 1950s, only a few voices were around to speak into my life compared to now. Advice and guidance came mainly from my parents, the church, schoolteachers and my friends. Now we get input from innumerable sources, and we have to decide what is valid. Voices from those around us can be tested rather easily by the fruit borne in those people's lives. Voices from outside our circle of friends and acquaintances—such as those on the Internet—present a different problem. It is sometimes hard to evaluate the source; even channels that bring us the news can have a hidden point of view. We need to listen to those proven correct over time.

The subject of prophecy invokes passion among Christians and brings up complex issues. The Bible is a prophetic book, and churches ought to have prophetic voices. While prophecy in the local body is primarily meant to build it up, it can also be predictive; when it is, it can be judged. But what about the great number of prophetic voices coming from outside the local church, such as from television, radio, books and the Internet? They may warn, for example, of a coming catastrophe. They may predict that the end is near, or that we should buy gold, grain or a foreign currency. Sometimes *they* will benefit if we respond; then the enemy uses wrong motives on our part to seduce us. Before accepting guidance that is said to come from the Lord, whether it was spoken locally or outside the local body, we ought to know the track record of the people who spoke it. Again, knowing the Bible helps us discern truth from error. The prophetic Word in Scripture has stood the test of time because it came to pass.

We all need good advisors, good counselors, who have been proven wise and consistent, and to care about our well-being. They do not advise merely for personal gain but because they care about us and will be there to help us if we err. These are the ones whose counsel we should not be quick to ignore.

Proverbs and Ecclesiastes, two wisdom books of the Bible, devote entire chapters to giving us counsel; in these books wisdom is valued above all else. Wisdom is the ability to discern the proper decisions and materials used to build a life that lasts. My parents, who were very wise, advocated my study of those books.

Acting in Obedience

We have discussed hearing from God and what to do when you believe that you have: Get sound counsel. There is yet another issue, however—obedience. Guidance should be examined, but ultimately, it is given so that we will act on it. "But be doers of the word, and not hearers only, deceiving yourselves" (James 1:22). If we hear but never act, we fall into a deception. We mistake knowing for doing.

When the Church transforms from a body into an "audience," it falls into deception, believing that knowing is doing. It is not. Audiences watch, listen and are entertained, but bodies act and function. The book of Acts is a book of *acts*, a record of how the apostles put the Word that they heard into motion. The contemporary Church needs a fresh study of the book of

Acts. We have fallen into what has often been called "analysis paralysis." Church members have become connoisseurs of good worship, good sermons and good programs. Often this has turned us into consumers rather than producers.

So the question becomes "What did I hear?" What counsel did I receive, and what did I *do* about it? Words have little force until acted upon.

The world has been changed by people who acted, whether they were good or evil. Evil triumphs when good people do nothing. If the Church awakens and acts, we will see the glory of God. If not, we will live in a world shaped by other forces. It is high time to awake to, hear and act on the Word of the Lord (Romans 13:11–14)!

There are times when the issues are so vital that we are called to fast. In the following chapter we will briefly discuss this important element in seriously seeking God.

Discussion Questions

1. Why is it important to receive counsel before acting?

2. Where should we *not* go for counsel? Why? (See Psalm 1:1.)

3. Where *should* we go for counsel?

4. Can you think of an occasion when you should have sought counsel but did not?

5. What good advice have you received? From whom?

6. What do you think of the process of hearing, getting counsel and then acting?

7. What are some dangers of unilateral action?

19

Should I Fast?

Under normal health conditions, fasting can be very beneficial physically, mentally and spiritually. My focus in this chapter will be on the latter. I encourage two things: Study materials on the subject, and if you have any health or medication issues, consult your physician.

I describe fasting as a voluntary denial of food, drink or pleasure in order to focus on a more important purpose. There are numerous types of fasts, from partial to total, for a brief period or longer. The primary issue in this chapter is our reason for fasting.

I well remember my first intentional fast. I attended a conference where I and another man were asked to pray for a disabled person. There was no immediate result, and the other man suggested we fast. It was not my idea, but I agreed. The next day we began the fast, and on that day I rode home from the conference with other friends, a five-hundred-mile journey. My travel partners brought loads of fried chicken, which they ate on the way, as I fasted. The car was full of the delicious aroma. I felt like malnutrition had set in after the first hundred miles.

Why Fast?

The fasting discussed in the Bible was usually associated with prayer and humbling before God, repentance from sin or some grave situation that required serious and unusual times of prayer. Fasting is designed to make it clear to God that we have humbled ourselves and are in need of His mercy.

Fasting for the purpose of appearing "spiritual" was clearly unacceptable to God (see Isaiah 58; Matthew 6:16–18). The same goes for any religious activity when the motivation for it is to be seen by men. Such activity is rooted in pride, not humility. Jesus advocated private fasting and prayer, as well as private giving (see Matthew 6:5–8, 16–18).

Fasting has a long history in Scripture. The Bible also implies fasting in some places where it is not specifically stated:

Moses fasted forty days on Mount Sinai (Deuteronomy 9:9) and commanded a fast on the solemn Day of Atonement (see Leviticus 23:27–29).

Hannah fasted while she prayed for a son (1 Samuel 1:7).

David fasted for the healing of his child, who nevertheless died (2 Samuel 12:16).

Esther called for a fast over the danger to her people (Esther 4:16).

Isaiah prophesied what an acceptable fast was in the sight of the Lord, along with the numerous rewards (Isaiah 58). We should all study this chapter.

Jesus fasted for forty days following His baptism and was led into the wilderness, where He was tempted by Satan. He did not command His disciples to fast but declared that they would after His departure (Matthew 9:14–17). He made it clear that His disciples would fast for reasons different from those of the Pharisees.

The leaders of the church in Antioch fasted prior to sending out Paul and Barnabas (Acts 13:1–3).

Though these examples show why and how people fasted, there are other examples of fasting in both the Old and New covenants. Daniel 9 is a great example of Daniel's fasting and confession of sin on behalf of Israel. Chapter 10 records that he engaged in a partial fast for 21 days (see Daniel 10:1–3). Anna was a widow and prophetess who served in the Temple with fasting and prayer. She was there when Mary and Joseph brought the baby Jesus and presented Him to the Lord.

Most religions practice some form of fasting, and Christians have practiced it in a variety of ways. Catholics and Orthodox Christians are told to fast on certain days and in certain ways, while evangelicals are left to their own discretion. In my view, we all need to better understand and practice fasting as evidence of our concern for the will of God and the needs of others. We need to humble ourselves before God, confess our sin and call out to God for our loved ones and others to know Jesus Christ as Lord.

Some Practical Aspects

Here are my suggestions as to how we should approach a fast. First, study the Bible in regard to fasting, specifically the purposes for biblical fasting. Read sound Bible teaching from trusted references as well. Next, I would consider any health issues that might be affected by a fast. If you are on a medication, consult your physician.

Purpose is important to a successful fast—wrong reasons are not effective. Fasting for dietary reasons may be physically helpful but not spiritually beneficial. Keep in mind that truly spiritual motives are humility, repentance and seeking the Lord.

I suggest deciding on a set amount of time before you begin, and begin small. Do not embark on a long fast until you have achieved a fast of shorter duration. Decide if your fast will be a partial or total one. Do not go for a long period without liquids.

Keep your fast private. Avoid discussion with others unless they will somehow be involved in the fast, or perhaps are close friends and family. Of course, a group fast or church-wide fast will include others.

It is good to prepare your body prior to fasting by eating less and drinking more. When you begin your fast, ask the Lord for help and be clear with Him about your reasons; keep your purpose before Him and yourself. Stay focused on the Lord and the purpose; it will help you endure.

You may see results during the fast, but in my experience results usually come later. Fasting is the time when we are sowing to the purpose. I do believe that during a fast our focus can become clearer, and the Lord's guidance can be received.

When the time comes to conclude the fast, do not overeat. A gradual return to normal eating is important. That is a good time to reflect on what you believe the Lord showed you about yourself and the purpose of your fast. We have numerous reasons to consider fasting; some are very serious. Our personal lives and relationship to God, families, churches, nation, neighbors, the poor and needy and those who are sick are additional reasons.

Fasting will probably not be easy (it is not for me), but the rewards of a rightly motivated fast can be life changing, for you and for others. My friend Julio Ruibal was a great evangelist in the nation of Colombia, filling large stadiums during his ministry. Julio gave his life serving the Lord; he preached against the drug lords and was murdered for his efforts. I heard him say, "Our greatest victories are won on our knees and with empty stomachs." Julio knew the results that came from fasting, and he also witnessed God's manifest presence in his life and ministry. We will consider the manifest presence of God in the next chapter.

Discussion Questions

1. What are some of the right reasons to fast?

2. What does "fasting" mean to you?

3. What are things to remember before you begin a fast?

4. Have you read Isaiah 58?

5. What are the possible results of God's "chosen" fast?

6. Do you regularly fast?

7. Do you believe that we should fast more often?

20

What Do You Mean by "the Manifest Presence of God"?

The Lord promised to be with us always, and He is always near in the Presence of His Holy Spirit (see Matthew 28:18–20; Hebrews 13:5–6; Acts 17:27–28). But there are times when His nearness is so clearly revealed as to be undeniable.

In 1975 I attended a men's conference in Kansas City, Missouri, where I witnessed such an occasion. My friend Ern Baxter brought the closing message, "Thy Kingdom Come." As he was finishing, all the men went down on their faces in humility at God's presence; then, after the meeting, they went throughout the city streets singing hymns and choruses—almost five thousand men. The manifest presence and power of God was evident and went with them into the city.

The Bible and history record many such examples of God's revealed presence, when all who were there responded. The good news is that as we seek Him, those occasions still happen. I recently prayed with a young man who had lived a rough life involved with drugs and alcohol. A few weeks earlier, he had given his life to Christ. As I prayed with him, he began to weep and tremble, and we both felt the presence of God.

Is this biblical? Absolutely. The patriarchs, Abraham, Isaac and Jacob, experienced such visitations of God's sovereign presence. The impact on each was profoundly life changing (see Genesis 15:1–16; 17:1; 18:1; 26:2–5; 28:10–22; 32:22–30). Moses and Joshua had their own encounters with the manifest presence of God. In fact, from Adam and Eve in the Garden until now, such occasions have continued to happen. I cannot explain it, but I have seen the presence of God on people as they ministered or as they were ministered to. I have witnessed a literal "glow," visible to my eyes. The results become evident in changed lives, healing or freedom from some bondage.

The biblical accounts of God's presence are too numerous to list here (Isaiah 6 and Revelation 1 are but two examples), and so are historical accounts outside the Bible. The evidences are always humility and revelation. Anyone who speaks casually or frivolously of such an experience is, at best, fabricating.

Entering God's Presence

I have sometimes found that when I focus on the Lord in deep gratitude, I become aware of His nearness. Or when I begin to worship Him, His presence becomes apparent. Recently I was driving to an appointment many miles away and thinking about how good the Lord had been to me for so many years, how He had preserved my life and poured out His blessings. Suddenly I became aware of His presence in the car. It was as though He was in the seat beside me. That awareness lasted for fifteen or twenty minutes.

Such an experience is humbling to me; had it intensified, I would have been undone! To think that the Creator of all that is, the Sovereign, would come near to us is an unimaginable grace. With God's revealed presence comes the holy awe of God, leaving us with a "limp" as it did Jacob (see Genesis 32:22–31).

The Bible often speaks of seeking God's face (see Psalm 27:8). That means seeking Him and His presence (see Numbers 6:22–26). We can enter the very presence of God if we seek Him, an amazing but real possibility. That is good to know when we are in times of trouble or danger. His presence resolves the issues and brings peace in the storm.

One of the most impressive accounts of the revealed presence of God occurred on a mountain when Jesus was transfigured in front of Peter, James and John, whom He had invited to join Him. Jesus' countenance and even His clothing became radiant; His face shone like the sun. The disciples were entranced by the amazing change:

> Then Peter answered and said to Jesus, "Lord, it is good for us to be here; if You wish, let us make here three tabernacles: one for You, one for Moses, and one for Elijah." While he was still speaking, behold, a bright cloud overshadowed them; and suddenly a voice came out of the cloud, saying, "This is My beloved Son, in whom I am well pleased. Hear Him!" And when the disciples heard it, they fell on their faces and were greatly afraid.
>
> Matthew 17:4–6

There is a lot to learn from this sacred event; two lessons are that we should remain humble and listen to Jesus. When He is talking, it is not the time for us to talk!

In my humble opinion, the highest goal of prayer is to know His revealed presence. Once we become aware, it is time to listen. There is much more to say about God's manifest presence, and I would encourage a more complete study of biblical accounts. But as I close this chapter, I pray that you have those moments when heaven comes down and calls you up into the eternal glory, where the reality of the realm of the Holy Spirit supersedes all earthly cares.

Peter, James and John had such moments, as did the other apostles and Paul. They were so affected that they gave their very lives for it—it was so real that they valued it more than their lives! Effective prayer is not just about getting an answer; it is about fellowship with our God in the Holy Spirit. That alone can sustain us, transform us and give us the peace and joy of His glorious Kingdom. Then a time will come when we enter His glorious presence and stay there forever! The closing chapter of this book will present wonderful examples of entering into eternal glory.

Discussion Questions

1. What does the manifest presence of God mean to you?

2. Why do we not experience it more often?

3. Have you had occasions when you knew beyond doubt that the Lord was near?

4. How did it affect you?

5. How did it affect the apostles?

6. What are some important steps to take toward His presence?

7. What are some results of His revealed presence?

21

How Can We Release Life to the Lord?

Life is precious and we must often fight for it, for our own lives and the lives of others. That is a natural instinct. But physical, mortal life is not permanent, and as believers we cannot enter our full inheritance in this body (see 1 Corinthians 15:50). In Philippians 1:21, Paul said, "To die is gain." There will come a time for each of us when we must release this life in order to enter the next. I suggest a study of 1 Corinthians 15 to learn about the victory in releasing our lives to Christ.

My purpose in this chapter is not to dwell on death but to illuminate our ability to release our lives to Christ in both life and death and know His peace and joy. Jesus taught His disciples this glorious truth by both His example on the cross and by precept. In our modern Western society, His instruction often seems remote and unreal in this regard. That is likely true because our culture is so focused on the physical to the neglect of the eternal.

I will offer several close, personal examples of the release of life into the peace of God. I have been a pastor for many years and have witnessed many departures and celebrations of life. I have seen very clearly that one's faith and fellowship with Jesus makes a profound difference. Facing that moment is no time to try to learn how to pray.

Jesus

Let us first look at Jesus' example of releasing His Spirit to the Father. We cannot comprehend the sufferings of Christ on the cross; besides the physical torture, mockery and rejection, there was the unimaginable burden of the sin of the world—our sin. In addition, He understood as no one else did the future cost to His beloved people for their rejection of God's offer of peace.

Isaiah 50 and 53 were written more than seven hundred years before the crucifixion, yet they give us an amazing account of the suffering that Jesus resolutely endured on our behalf. In the end His heart was broken but never bitter. Finally He said, "Father, into Your hands I commit My Spirit." He released His Spirit to the Father in peace, knowing that He had "finished" the Father's will.

I have seen documentaries on the Shroud of Turin, which many believe to be the actual burial cloth of Jesus. I cannot know if this is true, but it was evidently the burial cloth of a victim of crucifixion. What strikes me is the serenity on the face of the person it covered. I have never been impressed with artistic depictions of the face of Jesus, but I was impressed with the face captured on the shroud—it spoke of total, majestic peace, even in crucifixion!

Grandma Dix

Can one still find complete peace in the release of life? Yes, absolutely! The key is the kind of trust that brings a total release.

I mentioned my wife's grandmother earlier in this book; she died a few days short of turning 102. In her later years she broke her hip and was moved to a care facility. One day my wife's father, who was a physician, came by to see her, and she asked him, "Is any of my medicine strong enough to cause hallucinations?"

He answered, "No, why do you ask?"

"Well, there is a beautiful lady standing between my bed and the wall, but there is no room for anyone there."

My wife's mother, who had been reading Billy Graham's book on angels, visited Grandma Dix that same day. The "beautiful lady" was still there. That evening, my wife's grandmother had a small stroke and was moved to a hospital. Again my mother-in-law visited her and asked, "Is that beautiful lady still here with you?"

"Yes, she is," answered Grandma Dix, "and she is smiling." In a matter of minutes my wife's grandmother walked with the angel into God's eternal presence.

My Mother

I was Mother's firstborn, and she had me when she was still young, so we were close. Mother loved the Lord and her family deeply. She had a very tender heart but could speak the truth plainly, especially to those whom she loved. In 1991 she experienced kidney failure and required dialysis, which she hated. She would say more than once, "I want to go be with the Lord."

One night I went to my parents' home and was feeding Mom a meal-replacement shake. She did not want to eat. She looked me in the eyes and said, "Why don't you let me go? You are keeping me here, but I want to go be with the Lord."

I responded, "Okay, Mom, I'll release you." But I did not realize what that meant to her and to God. I prayed a brief prayer giving thanks to God for her and releasing her to Him.

It was very late in the night, so I went home to get some needed rest. I had hardly gotten in bed when the phone rang. Her night nurse told me, "Your mother has passed away; there was no struggle." I wish I had said more, much more, before she left us. I was so intent on keeping her that I had not said my final good-byes. That is when I learned the real meaning of release—but she understood it.

My Father

My father was a faithful minister for well over sixty years. He was also a wise and faithful father to me, my sister and my brother. I deeply regret that I was not with him at the moment of his leaving us; I was traveling in ministry. Our two sons helped care for him with great respect and compassion. Our daughter was working with children in Costa Rica. My older son, Stephen, who is also a pastor, was beside Dad's bed when he left us, and I will let him tell you what happened.

> My grandfather knew he was running the last few steps of his race. He was eager to go home to be with Jesus; he spoke often of heaven and also of being reunited with his beloved wife, Genoa, who had passed away six years before. His physical condition began to decline, and he was in hospice care. My brother, Jonathan, called me from Grandpa's bedside and told me that he did not know if Grandpa would live through the day. My brother had to go home for a little while, but I was already on my way to see Grandpa.
>
> When I arrived, the room was very quiet and bathed in the peace of God. My grandfather was sleeping, which I was glad to see, because he had been somewhat restless the previous few days. After checking on him, I sat beside his bed and began to silently pray and read his Bible, which was nearby. A few minutes passed before a doctor came in to check on Grandpa.

"He won't be with us much longer," the doctor said. When the doctor spoke, Grandpa opened his blue eyes, fixed them right on me, and he nodded his head.

I began to pray over him and tell him how much our family loved and honored him. I committed to him that we would carry on the godly legacy that he had entrusted to us. I sang the chorus of "Higher Ground," and then I read Psalm 23 and part of Romans 8. Grandpa breathed his last as I read aloud, "For I am persuaded that neither death nor life, nor angels nor principalities nor powers, nor things present nor things to come, nor height nor depth, nor any other created thing, shall be able to separate us from the love of God which is in Christ Jesus our Lord" (Romans 8:38–39).

It was as if Grandpa and I were walking together in God's presence, and then, at a certain point in the road, he was invited by the Holy Spirit to continue on to a place I could not yet go. It was glorious, and I was overcome by the joy of the Lord, even in the midst of sorrow in watching my grandfather pass away.

The peace of God lingered in the room, long after Grandpa left us. As other family members began to arrive, they sensed the Lord's presence as well. God's favor rested on His servant in life, in death and in eternity.

Carolyn

I am sure it is obvious that I still have difficulty describing my wife's passing into the presence of God. She went to heaven fifty years to the day of our first date. Like a lot of men, I married up! She was beautiful; she had a quiet spirit and a good heart. I cannot in this brief account adequately describe her, but she was always positive and supportive of me and our children. When I think of goodness, I think of Carolyn. At 68 years of age, suffering from ovarian cancer, she still looked years younger.

I used to kid her, "I am saving up money for your next husband," fully believing that she would outlive me by many years. But life is often defined by the unexpected. When we discovered her illness, it was in stage IV. We did everything humanly possible, both through prayer and medical help. I took her often to the MD Anderson Cancer Center in Houston and even to South Korea twice for adult stem cell treatment. We prolonged her life, but we could not save it.

Finally the moment of release came. We returned to the local hospital where she had been diagnosed, and family gathered. We all knew that it was time. There are no words—words are but tiny buckets that we dip into an ocean of emotion. We spoke of love, good times and the Lord's blessings. She had no pain, only peace. She told our granddaughter Grace, "I'm in the hands of Jesus now." I watched the monitors as her heart and breathing slowed. I released her to the One who loves her even more than we did; she nodded and went to sleep in His arms. The grief was deep, but I had a great peace knowing to whom and with whom she had gone. At her memorial her children called her "blessed" (see Proverbs 31:28).

I lived in our home for another year before moving in with my older son and his family. They have honored and cared for me as we did our parents before us.

My Father's Father

Let me give one more example of the release of life. My grandfather was a godly man who taught Sunday school for more than forty years. He was a deacon in the church and was elected sheriff of his county. Like my mother and Carolyn, his dear wife had passed on before him. And like Dad and I, he moved in with a son and daughter-in-law who cared for him with great kindness and respect.

Grandpa always kept a garden, and after tending the garden one evening, he came in for dinner. The family bowed their heads to say the blessing, but he never lifted his; he was with the Lord. What a way to meet the Lord in prayer!

Conclusion

I have witnessed many people passing into eternity; some struggled in pain and resistance. It was tragic to behold. Others were able to trust the One that they had found faithful in life. I have received many letters and comments about what one should do to keep their lives, but the most beautiful moments have been with those who knew how to give their lives.

One of my favorite verses is Revelation 12:11, "And they overcame him by the blood of the Lamb and by the word of their testimony, and they did not love their lives to the death." The hymn "Peace, Peace, Wonderful Peace" describes the peace of having this kind of trust in the Lord: "Far away in the depths of my spirit tonight, rolls a melody sweeter than psalm. In celestial strains it unceasingly falls o'er my soul like an infinite calm."

I hope that this book has blessed you and motivated you to deeper fellowship with our Lord in prayer. I leave you with my prayer that "the peace of God, which surpasses all understanding, will guard your hearts and minds through Christ Jesus" (Philippians 4:7).

Bibliography

Antonakis, John, Anna T. Cianciolo, and Robert J. Sternberg, eds. *The Nature of Leadership.* Thousand Oaks, Calif.: Sage, 2004.

Dallimore, Arnold A. *George Whitefield: The Life and Times of the Great Evangelist of the Eighteenth-Century Revival, Volume I.* 2nd ed. Westchester, Ill.: Cornerstone Books, 1980.

Dyck, Drew. *Generation Ex-Christian: Why Young Adults Are Leaving the Faith and How to Bring Them Back.* Chicago: Moody, 2010.

Gentile, Ernest B. *Your Sons and Daughters Shall Prophesy.* Grand Rapids, Mich.: Chosen Books, 1999.

Harris, Lyndon. "Sanctuary at Ground Zero." *National Geographic Magazine.* http://ngm.nationalgeographic.com/ngm/0209/st_pauls/online_extra.html.

Hayford, Jack, ed. *New Spirit-Filled Life Bible.* Nashville: Thomas Nelson Publishers, 1982.

Liardon, Roberts, ed. *Smith Wigglesworth: The Complete Collection of His Life Teachings.* New Kensington, Pa.: Whitaker House, 1996.

Mansfield, Stephen. *Never Give In.* Nashville: Cumberland House Publishing, 2000.

Price, Charles. *The Real Faith.* Pasadena: Charles S. Price Publishing, 1940.

Spalding, Matthew. *We Still Hold These Truths.* Wilmington, Del.: Intercollegiate Studies Institute, 2011.

Toffler, Alvin. *Future Shock*. New York: Bantam Books, 1971.

Washington, George. "Farewell Address," 1976. Lillian Goldman Law Library. http://avalon.law.yale.edu/18th_century/washing.asp.

Wessel, Helen, ed. *The Autobiography of Charles G. Finney*. Minneapolis: Bethany House, 1977.

Williamson, Porter B. *Patton's Principles*. Tucson: Management and Systems Consultants, Inc., 1979.

Rev. Charles Simpson is an internationally known author, Bible teacher, motivational speaker and pastor who has served in ministry since 1955. His humor and storytelling often carry a deeper message that is prophetic in its timeliness and timelessness.

Born in New Orleans in 1937, Charles grew up the son of a Baptist pastor in the bayous of Louisiana, and later in southern Alabama. He responded to God's call into ministry in 1955, at the age of eighteen; two years later he became the pastor of a Baptist church in Mobile, Alabama. He completed his bachelor's degree at William Carey College, Hattiesburg, Mississippi, in 1959, and attended New Orleans Baptist Theological Seminary.

In 1964 Charles experienced a profound personal spiritual renewal and began traveling and teaching in churches worldwide. He became widely recognized as a pioneer in the modern charismatic renewal movement. He was involved in the inaugural issue of *New Wine* magazine, an international publication dedicated to Christian growth, in 1969. During the next seventeen years, Charles wrote in and served alongside other notable Bible teachers on the board of *New Wine*, including Don Basham, Ern Baxter, Bob Mumford and Derek Prince.

Brother Charles and a team of pastors founded Covenant Church of Mobile in 1973, based on organic home cell groups centered on making disciples of Jesus Christ, serving communities and extending Christ's Kingdom around the world. In 1985, out of a strong ongoing emphasis on praise and worship, Covenant Church of Mobile and *New Wine* gave birth to Integrity Media, which became the largest praise and worship music company in the world. Charles served on Integrity's board of directors from 1985 to 2011, when Integrity Media became part of the David C. Cook company.

Charles Simpson is the author of numerous books, including *Courageous Living*, *The Challenge to Care* and *Ants, Vines and Churches*. He served as the senior editor of *The Covenant and the Kingdom* Bible study curriculum and contributed commentary for the popular *New Spirit-Filled Life Bible*. Charles received his honorary doctorate from the American Center for Theological Studies in 1998.

Today Charles serves as a spiritual father to many pastors and as a consultant to churches and businesses, traveling and ministering globally. He is editor-in-chief of *One-to-One* magazine and is a featured writer in every issue. Under the banner of CSM Publishing, *One-to-One* and its related website, audio recordings, videos, books and monthly pastoral letters reach around the world. For more information, please visit www.csmpublishing.org.

Charles resides in Mobile, Alabama. His wife of 47 years, Carolyn, went home to be with the Lord in 2008. Charles has three adult children and nine grandchildren.